UNITED STATE␣␣
K-TYPE AIRSHIPS

PILOT'S MANUAL

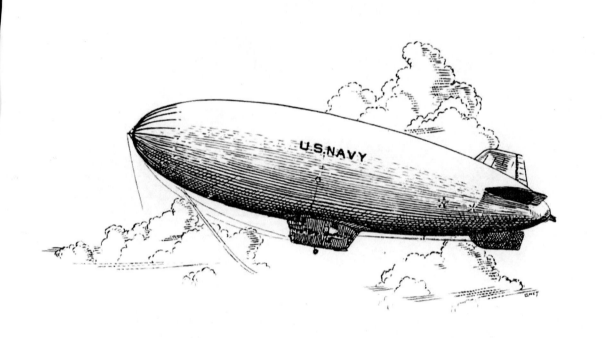

CONTRACTS NOs-78121 and NOa(s)-257

GOODYEAR AIRCRAFT CORPORATION
AKRON, OHIO

©2015 PERISCOPE FILM LLC
ALL RIGHTS RESERVED
ISBN #978-1-940453-35-4

First Issue: Sept., 1942
Revised Issue: Sept., 1943

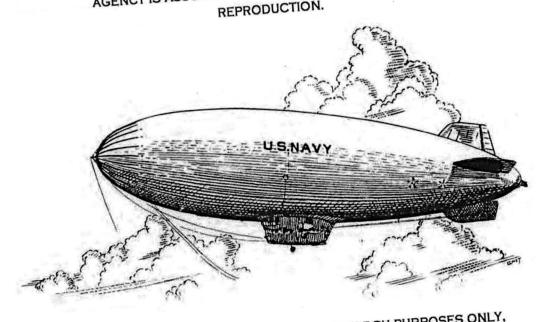

©2015 PERISCOPE FILM LLC
ALL RIGHTS RESERVED
ISBN #978-1-940453-35-4
WWW.PERISCOPEFILM.COM

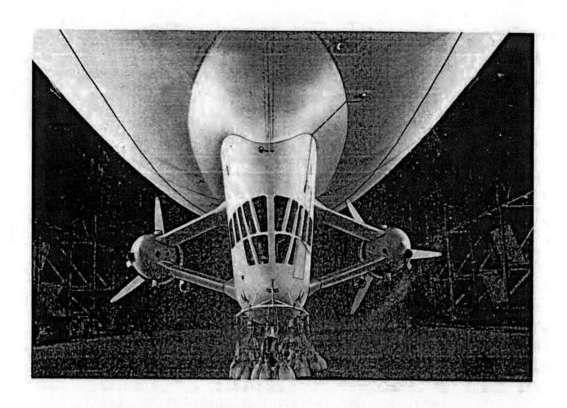

EXTRACT FROM ESPIONAGE ACT

"Section 31. Unlawfully obtaining or permitting to be obtained information effecting National Defense.***; or (d) whoever, lawfully or unlawfully having possession of, access to, control over, or being intrusted with any document, writing, code book, signal book, sketch, photograph, photographic negative, plan, blueprint, map, model, instrument, appliance, or note relating to the National Defense, willfully communicates or transmits or attempts to communicate or transmit the same to any person not entitled to receive it, or willfully retains the same and fails to deliver it on demand to the officer or employee of the United States entitled to receive it, or (e) whoever, being intrusted with or having lawful possession or control of any document, writing, code book, signal book, sketch, photograph, photographic negative, blueprint, plan, map, model, note, or information relating to the National Defense, through gross negligence permits the same to be removed from its proper place of custody or delivered to anyone in violation of his trust, or to be lost, stolen, abstracted or destroyed, shall be punished by a fine of not more than $10,000 or by imprisonment for not more than two years or both."

PREFACE

The information herein is designed to embody only such material as may be of value to the pilot and the crew of the K-airship during flight operations. Further descriptive matter vital to the ship and its care is set forth in the Specification and Maintenance Manuals.

While this manual is not intended to serve as an infallible guide for all flight operations, some of the more advanced points of aerostatics are included for ready reference.

Amendments will be made when significant changes in future airships occur.

The Goodyear Aircraft Corporation welcomes suggestions for the improvement of the airship and its equipment, and invites constructive criticism of this manual. Such suggestions will be cordially entertained and accorded the most careful consideration.

TABLE OF CONTENTS

Page

LIST OF ILLUSTRATIONS

Part I
General Description

GOODYEAR   K·AIRSHIP

A. DIMENSIONS AND CHARACTERISTICS

1. Overall Dimensions - Feet

	K-3 to K-13	K-14 & Future
Height	79.00	79.00
Width	62.50	62.50
Length	248.50	251.70

2. Envelope

Theoretical:

	K-3 to K-13	K-14 & Future
Volume, Cu.Ft.	416,000	425,000
Surface Area, Sq. Yds	3,900	3,965
Length, Ft.	246.00	249.20
Diameter, Ft.	57.85	57.85
Fineness or Slenderness Ratio	4.25	4.31
Maximum Section from Bow, Ft.	98.40	98.40
Center of Buoyancy, Ft.	112.40	113.95
Demonstrated Volume (with stretch) Cu. Ft.	424,600	435,000

3. Ballonets

	K-3 to K-6	K-7 to K-13	K-14 & Future
Volume - Cu.Ft.:			
Forward	55,700	53,000	58,950
Aft	58,400	58,400	61,600
Total	114,100	111,400	120,550
Per Cent Envelope Volume	27.5	26.8	27.7%
Surface Area - Sq. Yds.:			
Forward	544	525	544
Aft	562	562	562
Total	1106	1087	1106

4. Tail Surfaces - Sq. Ft.

	All Ships
Fins:	
Horizontal (2)	732
Top (1)	366
Bottom (1)	250
Total	1348
Rudders:	
Top (1)	130
Bottom (1)	69 *
Total	199
Elevators (2)	260
GRAND TOTAL - Tail Surfaces ..	1807

5. Weight and Lift - Lbs.

	K-3 to K-8	K-9 to K-13	K-14 & Future
Gross Lift (Based on 62 lbs. per 1000 Cu.Ft.with stretch)	26,325	26,325	26,970
Approximate Total Weight, Empty	17,600	18,350	18,430
Approximate Useful Lift ..	8,725	7,975	8,540
Ratio Useful Lift to Gross Lift	.331	.303	.310

6. Power Plants

K-3 to K-8: Engines (2) Wright, Model R-975-28, Direct
Drive-Horsepower, each 420 H.P. at 2200 RPM
Propellers (2) - Three Blades - 9'0" Diameter.

K-9 & Future: Engines (2) Pratt & Whitney Wasp, Model R-1340
-AN2, Geared 3:2
Horsepower, each - 425 H.P. at 1775 RPM
Propellers (2) - Three Blades - 12'0" Diameter

Propeller Pitch:	Diameter	Pitch Setting at 42" Station
	12'6"	19.5°
	12'0"	20.5°
	11'6"	21.5°

*Inboard aft corner cut to prevent
puncturing the envelope during
heavy landings.

B. AVERAGE PERFORMANCE *

	K-3 thru K-8			K-9 thru K-13			K-14 & Future		
Speed Knots	40	50.0	62.5	50	50	67.5	40	50	67.5
R.P.M.	1450	1780	2200	1120	1340	1775	1050	1290	1740
Fuel Consumption Lbs./Hour	120	160**	520	98	160**	375	102	165**	400
Endurance, Hours									
Based on 6000 Lbs.Fuel	50	37.5	11.5	-	-	-	-	-	-
" 5200 Lbs.Fuel	-	-	-	53.2	32.5	14	-	-	-
" 5650 Lbs.Fuel	-	-	-	-	-	-	55.0	34.2	14.1
Range, Nautical Miles ...	2000	1875	690	2130	1625	945	2200	1710	950

* See Pages 65, 66 and 67 for more complete performance data.

**Based on lean carburetor setting.

RECOMMENDED TOP SPEED - 67.5 KNOTS PER HOUR.

PART II
FLIGHT AND FLIGHT CONTROL

GOODYEAR   K·AIRSHIP

A. FLIGHT CHARACTERISTICS

The lift of an airship is made up of two components -- the static lift and the dynamic lift. These two components have different physical origins and require separat: treatment.

(1) Static Lift

The static lift is that component of lift which is due to buoyancy and which is independent of any motion of the ship with respect to the air.

The gross static lift of an airship is the difference between the weight of the air displaced and the weight of the lifting gas.

The net lift is the difference between the gross lift and the gross weight of the ship.

The ship is said to be "light" when the gross lift exceeds the gross weight. The ship is said to be "heavy" when the gross weight exceeds the gross lift.

In calculating the gross lift of an airship both the gas volume and the lift coefficient of the helium, or lift per 1000 cubic feet, must be known.

The lift coefficient can be computed, as indicated below, when various conditions of the atmosphere and of the helium are known.

The gas volume, however, can be determined accurately only when the ship is fully inflated. Calculations of gross lift are largely limited, therefore to full inflation.

Ordinarily an airship takes off less than fully inflated and the lift condition is determined by a weigh-off rather than by calculation. After take-off, the pilot is interested in keeping track of the variations in gross and net lift as affected by the burning of fuel or dropping of ballast on the one hand, and by the variations in atmospheric conditions on the other. The changes of lift can be followed by means of simple rules of thumb discussed later on.

(a) <u>Calculating Full Inflation Lift</u>

References: (1) War Department Technical Manual TM-135

(2) Goodyear Aircraft Report on 100% Weigh Off of K-4 Airship, Oct.15, 1941, Revised Nov. 6, 1943.

The lift coefficient, or lift per 1000 cubic feet can be computed from the following formula:

$$L = CP \left[\frac{1325 - 16.7\ Ra\ Ea}{Ta} - \frac{185 - 21.5\ Rg\ Eg}{Tg} \right] \quad (1)$$

Where: L = Lift Coefficient in lbs. per 1000 Cu.Ft.

C = Gas Purity, %

P = Atmospheric Pressure, in. of HG.

Ta = Absolute Air Temperature, °F.= 459.8 Plus Air Temp.

Tg = Absolute Gas Temperature, °F.= 459.8 Plus Gas Temp.

Ra = Relative Humidity of Air, %

Rg = Relative Humidity of Gas, %

Ea = Vapor Pressure at Temperature, Ta

Eg = Vapor Pressure at Temperature, Tg

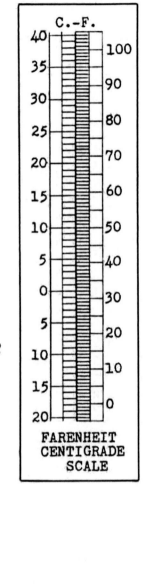

EFFECT °C. SUPERHEAT
ON LIFT

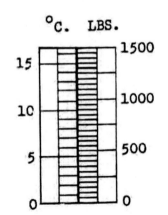

EFFECT °F. SUPERHEAT
ON LIFT

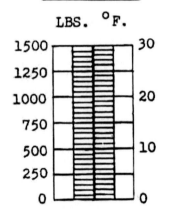

For K-Airship

Fig. I

Superheat Chart

If the effect of humidity is neglected, the formula becomes:

$$L = CP\left(\frac{1325}{T_a} - \frac{185}{T_g}\right) \qquad (2)$$

If $T_g = T_a$ and there is no superheat, then:

$$L = 1140\,\frac{CP}{T_a} \qquad (3)$$

Formula (3) may be accurate enough for rough computations. But even when more accurate results are desired, it may be found convenient to use this formula and to apply quick corrections for humidity and superheat according to the following rules:

1. For each 5° of positive superheat, increase lift by 1%.

2. For each 5° of negative superheat, reduce lift by 1%.

3. Correct for humidity in accordance with the following table:

LOSS IN LIFT CAUSED BY HUMIDITY

Air Temperature	Loss in Lift at Saturation
$0^\circ F$	1/20 of 1%
$20^\circ F$	1/10 of 1%
$32^\circ F$	1/5 of 1%
$50^\circ F$	1/2 of 1%
$70^\circ F$	1% less than dry air
$90^\circ F$	1.8% less than dry air
$100^\circ F$	2.5% less than dry air

For less than 100% humidity, multiply loss in lift at saturation by % humidity.

FIG. 21

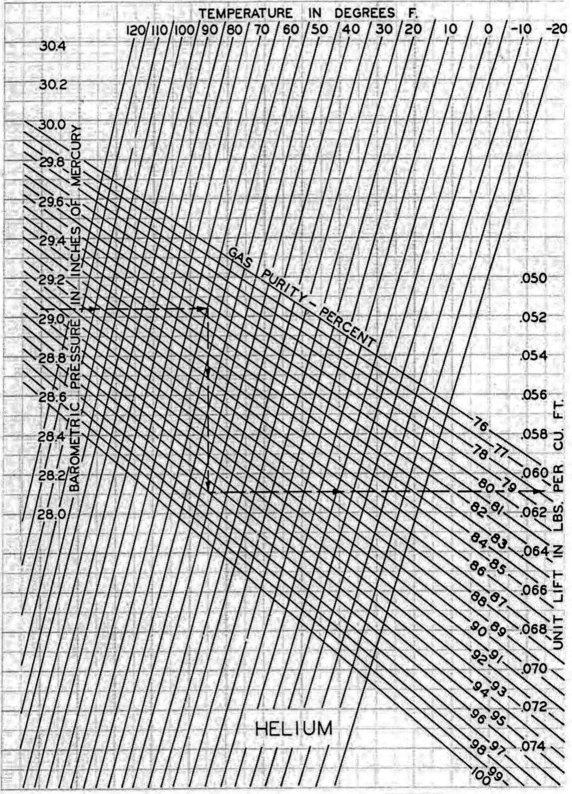

Fig. II - Helium Purity

The curves in Fig. II make it possible to find directly the lift coefficient given by formula (3). This lift coefficient should be corrected for humidity and superheat as outlined above.

(b) Lift Variations

The table below gives a number of rules which permit keeping track of lift variations after take-off.

EFFECT OF VARIOUS ATMOSPHERIC
CONDITIONS ON GROSS LIFT

CONDITION	EFFECT ON GROSS LIFT	
	Below Pressure Height	Above Pressure Height
Increased Altitude, Decreased Barometric Pressure	NONE	Reduced by 1% for every 360 ft.or .3 in. Hg. *
Decreased Altitude, Increased Barometric Pressure.	NONE	NONE **
Decreased Ambient Temperature, No Superheat	NONE	NONE **
Increased Ambient Temperature, No Superheat.	NONE	Reduced by 1% for every 5° F. *
Positive Superheat	Increased by 1% for every 5° F. *	Increased by a negligible amount.
Negative Superheat	Decreased by 1% for every 5° F. *	Decreased by 1% for every 5°F. **

* For the K-ship, 1% of gross lift amounts to about 250 lbs. Superheat can be seen, therefore, to affect lift by about 50 lbs. for every 1°F., or 90 lbs. for every 1°C.

** Gas contracts and ship is no longer at pressure height.

NOTE: The student pilot is sometimes confused by the apparent contradiction between some of the above rules, which seem to imply that lift is unaffected by temperature, and the known fact that an airship has a greater lift in winter than in summer.

The contradiction is easily cleared when it is considered that the rules in the above table apply only to the lift of an airship to which no helium is added.

It is true, as indicated by the above rules, that the lift of an airship inflated during the summer remains the same when cold weather sets in, provided no gas is added and no gas is lost and neglecting the effect of humidity. The gas and the displaced air contract in the same proportion so that a like weight of gas has the same lift in winter as in summer.

At the same time, because of the gas contraction, it is possible to add a certain amount of gas in winter to a ship which had been fully inflated in the summer. A fully inflated ship has, therefore, a greater lift in winter than in summer.

(2) Static Trim

An airship trims at an angle such as to bring the center of gravity directly below the center of buoyancy. The K-airships trim at an angle of 3.5°, plus or minus 1/2°, nose down at static equilibrium, when fully inflated, with conditions such as to produce a static lift of 62 lbs. per 1000 cubic feet and with a load distribution as indicated on the following page.

Under the above conditions, the location of the center of buoyancy and of some of the important centers of gravity along the longitudinal axis are given below:

Center of Buoyancy: 20.53 ft. Aft of Frame 9.

Center of Gravity of
Ship as a whole: 1.75 ft. Forward of Center of
Buoyancy.

Center of Gravity of
Loaded Car.   8.45 ft. Forward of Center of
Buoyancy.

Center of Gravity of
Envelope: 10.00 ft. Aft of Center of
Buoyancy.

The useful load is ordinarily distributed approximately about the center of gravity of the car so that changes in the useful load do not alter greatly the location of the center of gravity of the car.

The center of gravity of the ship as a whole, however, changes with the total car load since, as indicated above, the center of gravity of the car is considerably forward of the center of gravity of the envelope which makes up the balance of the gross load. An increase of car load has the effect of moving the center of gravity of the ship forward and of increasing the nose down angle. A decrease of car load has the effect of moving the center of gravity of the ship aft and of decreasing the nose down angle.

A change of 10,000 ft. lbs. in the moment balance with respect to the center of buoyancy of the ship, whether caused by a change of total load or by a change of load distribution, alters the static trim angle by about 1°.

Since the trim angle is measured at full inflation
and at equilibrium a change in the lift coefficient must be
accompanied by a corresponding change in the car load to
maintain equilibrium. Therefore, when the lift is greater,
the load will also be greater, and the ship will trim at a
greater nose down angle. A difference between the summer
and winter trim angles may be observed because of this factor.

At less than full inflation the trim of the ship is
affected by the above factors, and also by the relative
inflation of the ballonets.

(3) Dynamic Lift

The dynamic lift of an airship is the lift which depends upon the forward motion and the angle of attack of the
ship with respect to the air. See Fig. III for dynamic lift
at various forward speeds.

The curves plotted in Fig. IV show the variation of the
minimum length of the take-off run of model K-airships with
heaviness and head wind.

The assumptions on which the curves are based are
neither exact nor invariable, but they are on the safe side,
giving an over estimate rather than an under estimate of
the required length of the take-off run.

(4) Factors of Safety

The suspension system and the car structure of the K-
airship are designed for a total car load of 16,000 lbs. The
minimum factors of safety at this load are 3.00 for the car
structure and 4.00 for the car suspension.

-12-

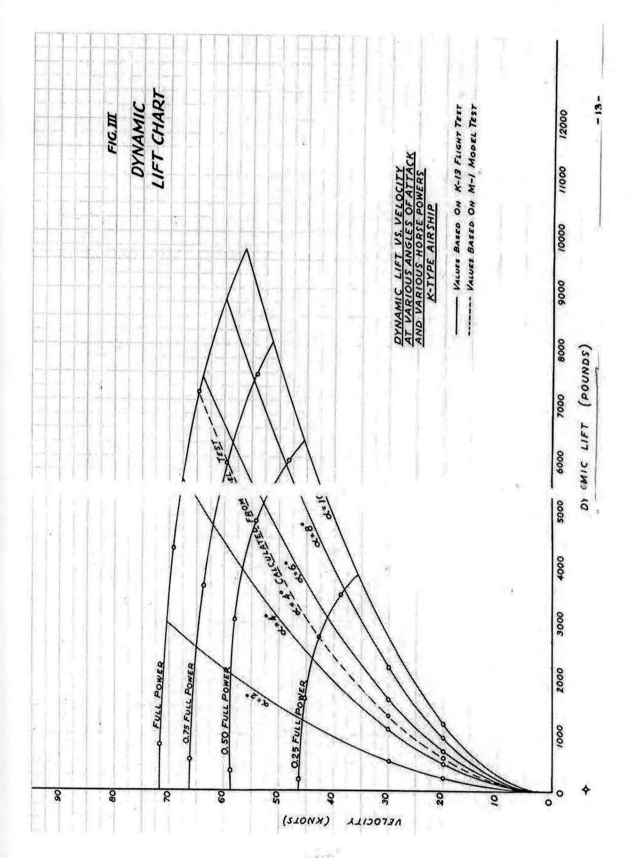

FIG. III

DYNAMIC
LIFT CHART

DYNAMIC LIFT VS. VELOCITY
AT VARIOUS ANGLES OF ATTACK
AND VARIOUS HORSE POWERS
K-TYPE AIRSHIP

—— VALUES BASED ON K-13 FLIGHT TEST
- - - VALUES BASED ON M-1 MODEL TEST

DYNAMIC LIFT (POUNDS)

VELOCITY (KNOTS)

FULL POWER

0.75 FULL POWER

0.50 FULL POWER

0.25 FULL POWER

CALCULATED FROM

$\alpha = 2°$
$\alpha = 4°$
$\alpha = 6°$
$\alpha = 8°$
$\alpha = 10°$

- 13 -

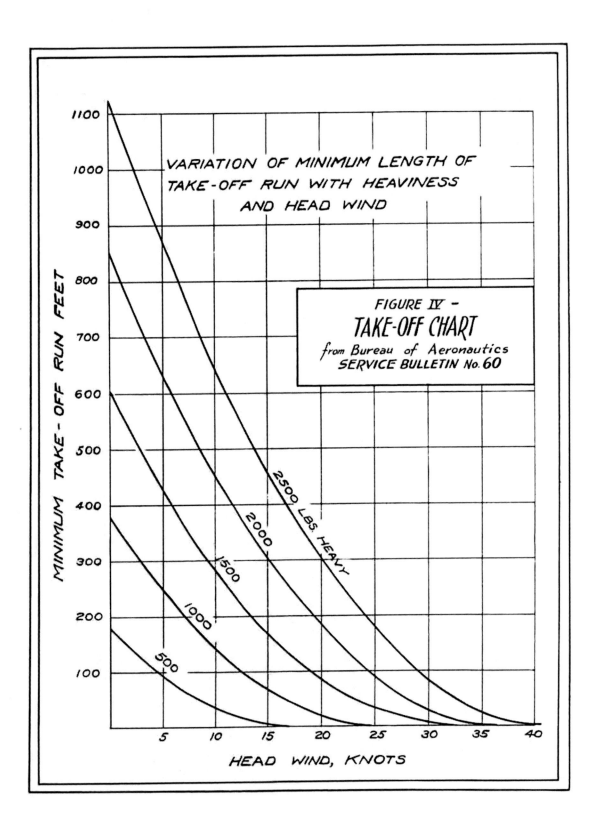

(5)   <u>WEIGHT EMPTY</u>

Note: All weights are for ships before K-75.

<u>ENVELOPE GROUP</u>

```
Main Envelope Fabric .............................    5670.4 Lbs.
Ballonets ........................................     820.0
Air Lines ........................................     195.3
        Frames ........................   85.7 Lbs.
        Fabric Patches & Lacing ..........  109.6
Rip Panels, Complete with cords ..................      21.1
Car Suspension ...................................     778.5
        Inside Catenaries ................  524.0
        Inside Cables  ..................  129.6
        Outside Catenaries .............  102.2
        Outside Cables  ................   22.7

Gas Valves & Reinforcement .......................      68.0
Air Pressure System ..............................       6.0
        Air Valve Reinforcement ..........    6.0

Bow Stiffening  ..................................     693.3
        Bow Cone .......................  106.8
        Batten Patches, Laces, Etc. .....  102.0
        Battens ........................  378.0
        Batten Cables ..................   28.6
        Mooring Cone Spindle & Pendant ...   45.4
        Miscellaneous ..................   32.5

Handling Lines ...................................     137.2
        Drag Rope ......................   18.5
        Yaw Lines ......................   39.9
        Handling Lines, All Others .......   78.8

Fin Suspension, attached to envelope .............     145.6
Lighting & Bonding System ........................      20.5
Car Fairing, Tape Lacing Cord & Padding ..........      31.8
Miscellaneous equipment, patches, manholes and
    sleeves attached to the envelope ...........     301.6

    TOTAL ENVELOPE GROUP .........................    8895.3 Lbs.
```

<u>EMPENNAGE GROUP</u>

```
        Upper Fin .......................  241.0 Lbs.
        Horizontal Fins (2) .............  482.0
        Lower Fin .......................  217.0
        Upper Rudder ....................   86.0
        Elevators (2) ...................  172.0
        Lower Rudder ....................   56.0
        Fin Brace System ................  100.0

    TOTAL EMPENNAGE GROUP .....................    1354.0 Lbs.

    TOTAL ENVELOPE & EMPENNAGE  ...............   10,249.3 Lbs.
```

-15-

WEIGHT EMPTY

CONTROL CAR GROUP

Car .... 2250.0 Lbs.
    Framework ....1056.0 Lbs.
    Metal Skin & Skin Stiffeners 436.6
    Fabric Covering 5.6
    Windows 120.1
    Doors Complete 61.1
    Handling Boxes and Doors 9.5
    Bomb Hatch Doors & Opening Mech. 44.6
    Hand Rails and Brackets 32.7
    Insulation & Compartment Partition 33.8
    Flooring & Supports 322.6
    Access Ladders if carried in flight 16.8
    Miscellaneous 110.6

Landing Gear
    Landing Wheel Assembly .... 228.5 Lbs.
    Wheel & Tire .... 77.5 Lbs.
    Fork and Axle 45.9
    Shock Absorber 43.6
    Retracting Mechanism 37.5
    Miscellaneous Installation 24.0

Outriggers & Engine Nacelles .... 741.1 Lbs.
    Structure .... 250.0 Lbs.
    Metal Skin & Skin Stiffeners 151.5
    Engine Mounts 78.8
    Cowlings 95.0
    Engine Nacelles & Stiffeners 165.8

Power Plant Group .... 2642.8 Lbs.
    Engines (as installed) .... 1858.0 Lbs.
    Engine Accessories 238.1
    Power Plant Controls 39.9
    Propellers 422.8
    Starting System 84.0

Lubrication System .... 154.3 Lbs.
    Tanks & Protection, Installation 44.1 Lbs.
    Oil Coolers 60.5
    Pumps, not integral with engine 4.5
    Piping, etc. 45.2

WEIGHT EMPTY

Fuel System .... 548.0 Lbs.
    Tanks & Protection, installation
    Pumps, including transfer pump &
    hose .... 314.4 Lbs.
    Piping for Fuel and Vent Systems 233.6

Fixed Equipment .... 2050.9 Lbs.
    Instruments .... 127.2 Lbs.
    Major Controls, complete 125.8
    Minor Controls, complete 42.5
    Pressure Tube Assembly 32.6
    Electrical 624.8
    Communication (Radio & Radar,
            MAD, IFF) 1098.0

Furnishings .... 466.9 Lbs.
    Personnel .... 287.4 Lbs.
    Emergency 47.4
    Chair Base in Aft Section 3.2
    Navigator's Table 19.9
    Radio Table 26.7
    Heating Equipment 33.0
    Car Ceiling 27.3
    Rigger's Cabinet 15.0
    Navigational Gear Rack 5.3
    Miscellaneous 1.7

Air System .... 352.8 Lbs.

Auxiliary Power Plant .... 200.3 Lbs.

                     TOTAL CAR GROUP .... 9635.6 Lbs.

(6)   <u>USEFUL LOAD</u>

Crew (10 Men at 175 lbs. each) .... 1750.0 Lbs.

Fuel -
    Main Engines & Aux. Engines .... 3930.0 Lbs.
    Overhead Tanks 475 Gal.@ 6#/Gal. 2850.0 Lbs.
    Slip Tanks, 180 Gal. 1080.0

Oil -
    Main Engines - 52 Gal. @ 7.5# Gal. ....   390.0 Lbs.
    Aux. Power Plant, 3 Gal. @ 7.5# 22.5

Droppable Fuel Tanks (2) ....   42.1 Lbs.

Baggage ....   00.0 Lbs.

Cargo ....   00.0 Lbs.

Armament .... 1620.0 Lbs.

    1. 50 Cal. M.G. ....   105.0 Lbs.
    2. M.G. Ammunition 132.0
    3. Bomb Racks (2) 41.6
    4. Bomb Racks (2) 41.6
    5. Bombs M-17 (2) 650.0
    6. Bombs M-17 (2) 650.0

Equipment ....   570.3 Lbs.

Navigation Gear
    a. Charts, Publications ......   7.5 Lbs.
    b. Optical Drift Sight 13.5
    c. Wiley Drift Sight 1.5
    d. Parallel Rulers, Binoculars,
       Stop Watch, Dividers 14.0
    e. Miscellaneous Gear 18.5

                    Total   55.0 Lbs.

    Photographic ....   55.0 Lbs.

    Pyrotechnics -

    a. Signal Pistol ....   2.1 Lbs.
    b. 24 Rounds Signal Flares 7.2
    c. 24 Float Lights 52.8
    d. 24 Bronze Powder Markers ...   48.0

                    Total   110.1 Lbs.

USEFUL LOAD

Emergency Life Saving Equipment:

    a. Ten Life Jackets @ 3# .... 30.0 Lbs.
    b. Life Raft .... <u>66.0</u>

                     Total .... 96.0 Lbs.

Food and Water:

    a. Food, Canned .... 30.0 Lbs.
    b. Food, Fresh 55.0
    c. Water, Fresh 35.0
    d. Rescue, Rations 16.0
    e. Emergency, Food and Water ...... <u>27.0</u>

                     Total   163.0 Lbs.

Miscellaneous Equipment:

    a. Classified Container .... 2.2 Lbs.
    b. Emergency Cable 5.0
    c. Two Flashlights @ 3/4 Lbs. 1.5
    d. Signal Flags 1.0
    e. Fuel Pick-up, Green Marker Buoys,
       Grapnel 28.0
    f. One (1) Chute, One (1) Harness .. 18.0
    g. P. & W. Engine Kit 15.0
    h. Wire Cutter and Knife 5.0
    i. Rigger's Kit .... <u>15.5</u>

                   Total   91.2 Lbs.

                 TOTAL USEFUL LOAD   8325.1 Lbs.

It is recommended that the total car load be not allowed to exceed 18,300 lbs., or 2300 lbs. over the design load.   Under such condition of 2300 lbs. "Design Heaviness" the factors of safety are reduced to about 2.6 for the car structure and about 3.5 for the car suspension.

NOTE: "Design heaviness" is the excess of car load over design load and should not be confused with "flight heaviness" which is the excess of gross load over gross lift.

"Flight heaviness" alone is no measure of the factors of safety of the car structure and suspension.

Under conditions of high lift there may be no "flight heaviness" but a high "design heaviness."

Under conditions of low lift there may be no "design heaviness" but a high "flight heaviness."

Preceeding pages show computations of a typical car load.   It is suggested that similar forms be used for actual computations before take-off.

B. ENVELOPE PRESSURE CONTROL SYSTEM

(1) General Description

The maintenance of a predetermined pressure differential between the gas in the envelope of a non-rigid airship and the surrounding atmosphere is the first basic requirement to the successful operation of this type of airship.

The functioning of the envelope in assuming the various flight stresses, the proper suspension of the car, the efficient operation of the controls, all depend upon a closely held pressure differential.

It is the function of the pressure control system to maintain this pressure differential within a certain range and to do this with a minimum loss of lifting gas. This result is accomplished by inflating the envelope partly with gas and partly with air, the air being contained in a forward and an aft ballonet, and by regulating the inflation of the air by means of an air system, without changes to the amount of gas in the envelope. Under extreme conditions, outside of the range of the air system, gas can be released automatically by means of two gas valves to prevent the internal pressure of the envelope from rising above a safe value.

The pressure control system is also used to adjust the trim of the ship by regulating the relative inflation of the two ballonets.

(2) <u>Air System</u>

The air system comprises a forward and an aft ballonet, a system of scoops, ducts, valves and air chambers. Air is taken in at scoops located in the port and starboard motor outriggers and is led through a check valve of the butterfly type into an air chamber. From this chamber, two air ducts lead, one to the forward and the other to the aft ballonet, through manually controlled dampers. An automatic valve is connected to each ballonet system and is set to release air automatically when the pressure reaches a pre-determined value. In airships K-3 thru K-98, a blower with a gasoline power plant is provided in the cabin to supply pressure to the air system when the pressure from the regular system becomes inadequate. In airships K-99 and future, an electric blower is provided. The construction of the system is described in full detail in the "Descriptive Specifications Manual." The operation of the system is considered further below:

(a) <u>Scoops</u>

As mentioned above, air is collected by scoops located in the port and the starboard outrigger and is led to an air chamber through check valves. This air chamber can be connected to either or both ballonets by means of two manually controlled dampers. The air pressure in the ballonets can be adjusted within certain limits, as described further on, by regulating the opening of the scoops.

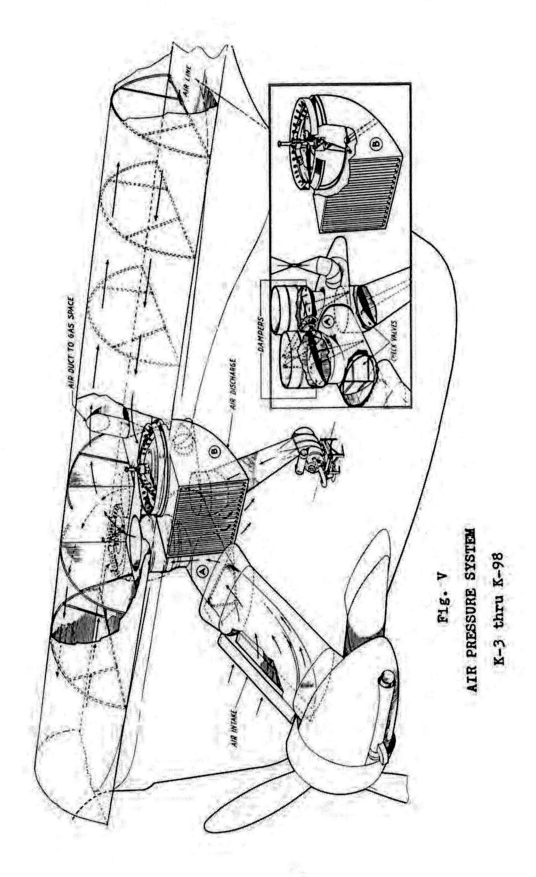

Fig. V

AIR PRESSURE SYSTEM

K-3 thru K-98

Fig. VI   Air Scoops

(b) <u>Valve Settings</u>   (See Buaer Manual 12-304)

The pressure in the forward and aft ballonets is limited by the forward and aft automatic air release valves. These
two valves are set to operate at different pressures for
reasons that will become apparent further on.

The valve of the forward ballonet is set to start opening when the air pressure in the forward ballonet, as read
at the car manometer, reaches 1.50 inches of water. The
valve of the aft ballonet is set to begin to open at an air
pressure of 2.00 inches of water.

When the ballonets are partly inflated there is a
difference of pressure between the air in the ballonets and
the gas in the envelope. This difference depends upon the

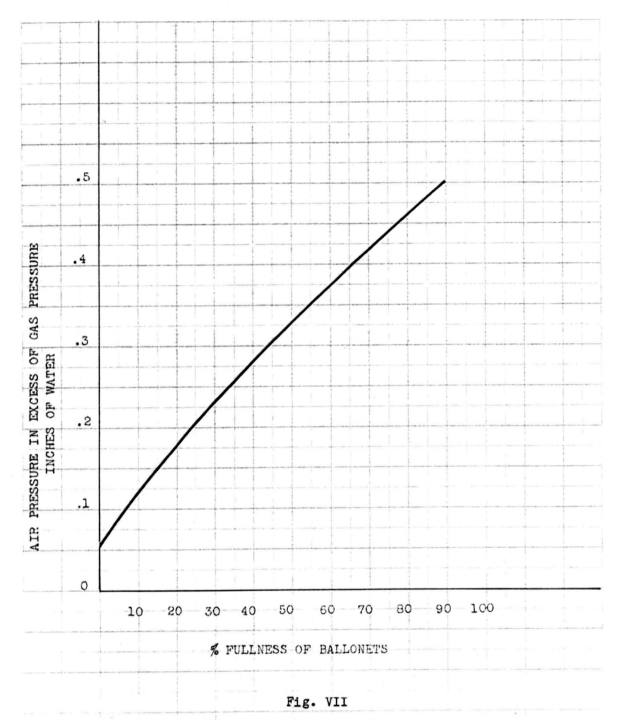

Fig. VII

AIR PRESSURE IN EXCESS OF GAS PRESSURE
VS
% FULLNESS OF BALLONETS AT ZERO PITCH ANGLE
AT STANDARD UNIT LIFT CONDITIONS

height of the upper part of the fabric of the ballonets
or upon the degree of their inflations, upon the lift coefficient of the gas, and upon the fabric weight which
reacts on the air.

Curve in Fig. VII shows the relation between this
difference in pressure and the inflation of the ballonets
at standard lift coefficient. It will be noted that the
difference of pressure is about 0.50 inches at full inflation and nearly zero when the ballonets are fully deflated.

Since the automatic air valves are operated by the
air pressure in the ballonets and not by the gas pressure,
it will be obvious that the system will tend to regulate
for a higher gas pressure when the ballonets are empty than
when they are inflated.

(c) Pressure Regulation

Under normal flight condition a gas pressure of about
1.5 inches of water should be maintained with a maximum variation of 1.25 to 2.00 inches.

CAUTION: Under no condition should the pressure be allowed
to go lower than 0.5 inch or higher than 3.0 inches
of water, the lower pressure being permissible only
in landing operations or in the hangar when there
is little or no forward speed.

It is particularly essential to maintain an adequate
internal pressure when the ship is operated at high speed
or when moored at the mast during high winds.

The K-airships are designed for a maximum speed of 65 knots with an internal gas pressure of 1.5 inches of water.

Since the automatic air valves, as pointed out above, are operated by the air pressure of the ballonets, the corresponding gas pressure at which they open depends on the gas inflation of the ship. If, for instance, the ship is 85% gas inflated and the ballonets are more than half inflated, it can be seen, by referring to the curve in Fig. VII that the gas pressure in the envelope is about 0.32 inches of water less than the air pressure in the ballonets. The air valve of the forward ballonet will open, therefore, at air pressure of 1.5 inches of water, while the corresponding gas pressure is .32 inches of water less than the setting of the gas valve or 1.18 inches.

It will still be possible, however, to maintain the recommended operating gas pressure of 1.5 inches of water by opening the forward air damper and regulating the scoop opening so as to produce air circulation through the air damper and the partially opened air valve.

CAUTION: The matter of the proper regulation of the air scoops is of the utmost importance. If the scoops are opened too wide, excessive pressure may be built up in the envelope causing loss of gas. If the scoops are not opened enough, the gas pressure may drop to a dangerously low value resulting in buckling of the envelope.

With the differential valve setting outlined above, it is apparent that as long as the ship is operated below the pressure height of the forward ballonet, air is released only from this ballonet when the altitude of the ship is increased. Hence, if upon descending, the pilot operates only the forward damper, the air which has been valved out during the ascent will be replaced to the forward ballonet, thus restoring the trim of the ship to the same condition that existed at take-off.

During short flights, the operation of the system is automatic, and no manual adjustment needs to be made except to open the forward damper. During long flights, occasional manual adjustments of the air balance may be necessary, but the system remains largely self-operating.

(d) Air Valve Adjustment

All valves are adjusted to their specified settings and tested before being installed in the airship and retested after installation.

The valve settings should not be changed unless difficulties arise. Adjustments should then be made only by a qualified person. During emergency, it may be necessary to adjust the valve in flight. Instructions below should clarify any difficulties that may be encountered.

Two 36-inch diameter air valves, see Fig. VIII and IX, are provided in the air line in the top of the car structure for valving air from the ballonets. One of the valves is located between Frames 4 and 5, and valves air from the aft ballonet, the air going out through louvers on the port side of the car. The other valve, located between frames 6 and 7, valves air from the forward ballonet and exhausts air on the starboard side of the car. Control lines for opening and closing the valves extend to Pilot's Instrument panel, see Fig. XI, Page 42.

The air valves are set to open as follows:

Aft Valve -   2.0" H_2O

Forward Valve - 1.5" H_2O

To adjust valves on K-3 thru K-53, exclusive of K-49:

(1) Inside knob adjustments (Three)

(a) Break seal on each valve adjustment knob.
(b) Apply same number of turns to each knob. Never adjust one or two knobs, but adjust them all equally, to prevent warping and improper seating.
(c) One complete turn of each of the inside adjustments will effect a change in the opening point of .018 inch H_2O.
(d) Do all loosening and some tightening on the inside.
(e) Turn adjustments clockwise to tighten or increase opening pressure.
(f) Turn adjustments counter-clockwise to loosen or decrease opening pressure.
(g) Re-seal valve adjustments to prevent valve from losing its setting.

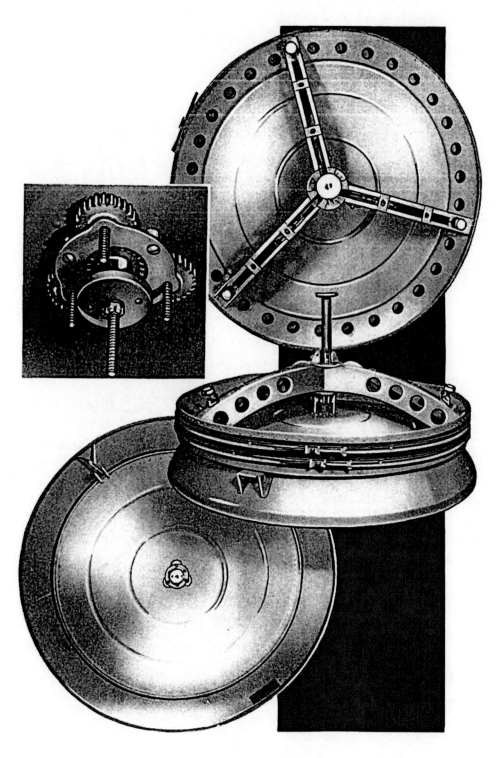

Fig. VIII - 36" Air Valve
K-3 thru K-53, Excl. of K-49

(2) Outside Gear Adjustments

    (a) Remove gear cover.
    (b) Remove cotter pin (through gear).
    (c) Do most tightening on outside gear and no loosening.
    (d) When tightened until 2-7/8" of screw protrudes from the gear, the forward or aft air valve opening point will increase 7/16" H_2O. This is a maximum condition.
    (e) Turn counter-clockwise to tighten or increase opening point.
    (f) Turn clockwise to loosen or decrease opening point.
    (g) Replace cotter pin and gear cover.

In the event the valves are completely out of adjustment, then proceed as follows:

    1. Set outside gear adjustment to neutral setting.

        NOTE: Neutral setting is defined as 1-1/2" of screw protrusion from gear. Total length of screw is 3 inches.

    2. Build up air pressure to 1.5" H_2O at the manometer in the car and adjust inside knobs as previously described.

    3. The valve is considered in adjustment when the dome begins to float freely and emits a characteristic hum.

    4. Re-seal all adjustment knobs and replace outside adjusting gear cover, together with the cotter pin.

    Insofar as the aft valve is concerned, build up air pressure to 2 inches and repeat the above procedure.

To adjust valves on K-49, K-54 and later airships:

Open the zippers for the access openings in the ceiling of the car and remove the lock seal attached to each knob. Unscrew the 1/2" O.D. sealing caps and turn adjusting knobs.

Give each of the knobs an equal number of turns and in the same direction. Turning the knobs clockwise, or to the right, increases the pressure necessary to operate the valve. Turning the knobs counter-clockwise, or to the left, lowers the pressure necessary to operate the valve. Tests conducted on a number of modified valves in a valve test chamber determined that ten complete turns on each of the three knobs changes the pressure setting necessary to operate the valve by 1/5 of an inch of H_2O.

After a satisfactory resetting is found, add leather washers and screw the sealing caps in place again, then safety the knobs to the clips on the shield. Test setting against the air manometers. The use of the gas manometer is misleading, except at, or very near, pressure height.

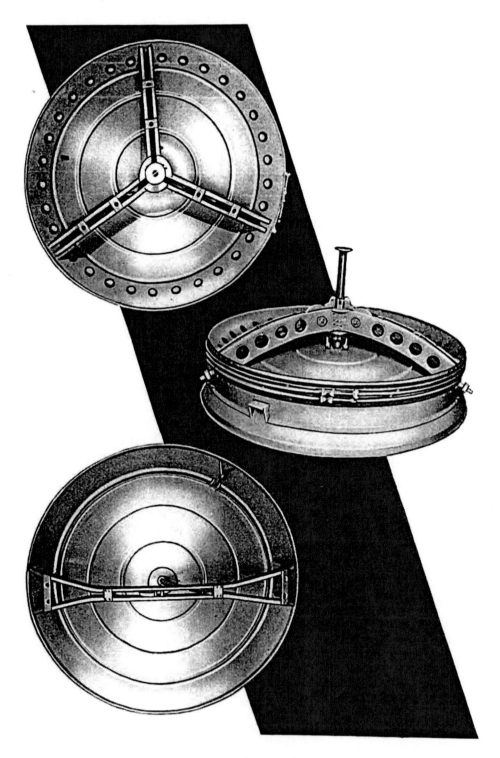

Fig. IX - 36" Air Valve
K-49, K-54 & Future

(e) Take-Off

When the ship is in the hangar it is normally kept under proper pressure by means of a ground blower. As the ship is taken out of the hangar, weather conditions may be such as to cause a change of the temperature of the gas.

If the temperature is increased, air will be released automatically by the air valves. If the temperature is decreased, air may have to be blown into the system to keep up the pressure. This may be done by opening the scoops and the air dampers, and speeding up the engines or it may be done by means of the auxiliary blower.

NOTE: The dampers can be kept continuously open while air is blown occasionally in the system by maneuvering the throttles, the check valves preventing loss of air when the engines are idle. Under normal conditions, however, it is best to keep the dampers closed when not pumping air.

(f) Climb

As soon as the ship begins to rise, the problem is no longer one of feeding air to the system, but one of releasing air to maintain a constant differential pressure between the gas in the envelope and the decreasing atmospheric pressure. This is done automatically as outlined above, by the air valves. The air valves and ducts can prevent the pressure from rising above 2.5 inches of water when the ship is rising at a speed of 2400 ft. per minute.

During the climb both dampers should be closed. The scoops, however, should remain open so that the pilot may be able to blow air into the ballonets by opening the dampers, should he decide to come down again.

CAUTION: 2400 ft. per minute is the maximum permissible rate of climb. The actual rate of climb should be kept well below this value.

(g) Level Flight

In level flight it is common practice to keep the forward damper and the scoops open so as to produce an air pressure slightly higher than the setting of the valves, causing a circulation of air through the air damper and the air valve.

CAUTION: The air release valves should not be opened manually when the ship is flying near or above pressure height.

A warning to this effect is mounted on the pilot's instrument panel. As long as the valves are operated automatically, with the scoops and air damper opened, pressure in the system does not drop below the setting of the valves although the ballonets may become completely deflated. If the air valves were opened manually at this point, the small amount of air in the system would become quickly exhausted, the pressure dropping to atmospheric pressure. The air line patches or the air line frame may be damaged by the full unbalanced gas pressure.

(h) Descending

When the ship is descending, air must be fed into the system to maintain the differential pressure between the inside of the envelope and the increasing atmospheric pressure. The scoops should be opened wide enough to permit adequate air flow. The air scoops, ducts, and damper valves can admit air into the ballonets at a sufficient rate to maintain a gas pressure of 1.25 inches of water when the ship is descending at a rate of 1200 feet per minute, at a forward speed of 50 knots.

The air intake capacity naturally decreases as the forward speed is reduced so that the maximum permissible rate of descent is less than 1200 feet per minute when the forward speed is less than 50 knots.

CAUTION: 1200 feet per minute is the maximum permissible rate of descent. The actual rate of descent should be kept well below this value.

(i) Landing

At the time of landing it usually becomes necessary to throttle down the motors and the air scoop system can no longer supply the required pressure to the ballonets. An auxiliary blower is provided for such conditions.

The blower is of sufficient capacity to maintain a gas pressure of 0.5 inches of water at the gas manometer

when the ship is descending without power at the rate of
250 ft. per minute. This pressure, while inadequate for
normal flight, is sufficient to permit satisfactory handling of the ship during landing operations.

Instructions for starting the blower for airships
K-3 thru K-98 are given on page 44.

(j) Shifting Air

During flight, it may become necessary to adjust the
relative inflation of the two ballonets in order to change
the trim of the ship. This is done by operating the air
valves and dampers manually.

In trimming the ship in this manner, it may be well to
consider air as ordinary ballast, the effect of transferring
air being the same as that of transferring any ballast.

(k) Blowing Air Into The Gas

In emergency cases where a large amount of gas has been
lost, such as when the ship is descending after having over-
shot its pressure height, and the ballonets, even when fully
inflated, cannot keep up the pressure of the envelope, it
may become necessary to blow air into the gas.

This may be done by untying the sleeve connecting the
air chamber to the envelope. This sleeve is located above

the cabin ceiling, starboard, and makes a "Y" connection with the helium inflation sleeve. Only the amount of air necessary to bring the pressure to the required value should be used.

(3) <u>Gas Release System</u>   (See BuAer Manual 12-304 12-307).

The gas release system includes two 20-inch gas valves, located on the port and starboard sides of the envelope at panel 34, and gores K and L. It includes, also, two rip panels located on the top of the ship from panel 21 to 28, and from panel 53 to 59.

(a) <u>Gas Valves</u>

The gas valves are set to operate automatically when the gas pressure reaches 2-1/2-inches of water as read on the gas manometer. They can also be operated manually from the pilot's instrument panel. The gas valves are equipped with micro switches which operate telltale lights on the pilot's panel when the gas valve begins to open at 2-1/2-inches of water. In order to offset localized drop of pressure in the air stream and to prevent premature opening of the valves, a semi-circular windshield is attached to the envelope on the aft side of the valve.

CAUTION: <u>Do not attempt to hold gas valves closed manually when flying above pressure height as excessive pressure may develop in the envelope</u>.

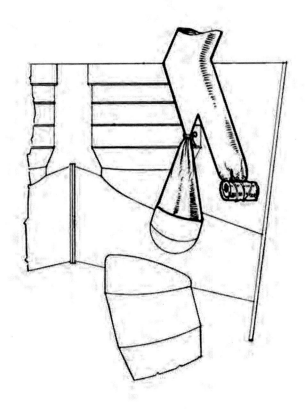

Fig. X

Helium Inflation Sleeve

(b) Rip Panels

The rope which opens the forward rip panel can be reached from the forward door; the rope which opens the aft panel can be reached from the aft door. They are dyed red to avoid confusion with the other ropes.

(4) Controls and Auxiliaries

(a) Valve Controls

The air and gas release valves can be operated manually from the pilot's instrument panel, Fig. XI. Every valve has an opening and a closing control. Pulling the opening control lifts the valve off its seat and releases air or gas as the case may be. The valves should close by themselves when the opening control is released.

A closing control is provided, however, to force the valves closed in case they should stick. The control is also used to make certain that the gas valves are closed, and that no gas is being lost when flying near pressure height.

The following check procedure of the valves is recommended:

1. Before take-off, crack all valves open for a short instant to make certain that the valves and telltale lights operate satisfactorily.

2. When flying close to pressure height, pull closing control of gas valves from time to time.

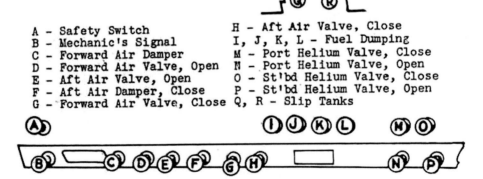

A - Safety Switch   H - Aft Air Valve, Close
B - Mechanic's Signal   I, J, K, L - Fuel Dumping
C - Forward Air Damper   M - Port Helium Valve, Close
D - Forward Air Valve, Open N - Port Helium Valve, Open
E - Aft Air Valve, Open   O - St'bd Helium Valve, Close
F - Aft Air Damper, Close   P - St'bd Helium Valve, Open
G - Forward Air Valve, Close Q, R - Slip Tanks

Fig. XI - Flight and Instrument Panel

(b) <u>Damper Control</u>

The air dampers can be kept open by means of an olive on the control cables. The dampers are normally held closed by springs which prevent the dampers from opening under the pressure of air from the scoops.

(c) <u>Manometers</u>

The air pressure in the two ballonets and the gas pressure in the envelope are read on three manometers, located on the flight panel. Each manometer is equipped with a three-position valve.

When this valve is turned on the position marked "Check" the manometers should read zero. If necessary, the reading can be brought back to zero by means of an adjusting dial. This check should be made before every take-off.

While in flight the valve should be turned on the position marked "static."

A mechanical manometer on the instrument panel reads the gas pressure and is used as a check on the liquid manometer.

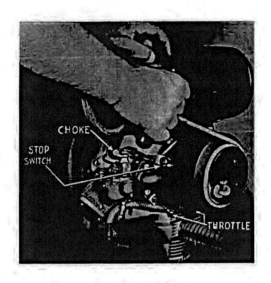

Fig. XII
Starting Auxiliary Blower
(K-3 thru K-98)

(d) <u>Starting Auxiliary Blower</u>   (K-3 thru K-98)

1. Turn on switch on pilot's instrument panel.

2. Open fuel line shut-off cock on gasoline
    filter bowl assembly. (Turn counter-clockwise).

3. Close carburetor choke (choke is open when
    lever is against stop pin). Open throttle
    by pulling black button on throttle wire.

4. Wind starting rope on pulley, brace one hand
    on fuel tank and pull rope hard, giving quick
    spin to engine. Repeat, if necessary, until
    engine starts. Then immediately open choke
    partially easing to full position as engine
    warms up. If engine is warm from previous
    running, it is not necessary to use choke for
    starting.

5. Open air intake door.

(e) Stopping Blower

      1. Turn off button on pilot's panel.

         NOTE: Engine can also be stopped by pressing
              red stop button, mounted on magneto
              stator plate until engine stops.

      2. When the airship is in flight with the Homelite
         Model HRU-28 auxiliary blower stopped, a
         partial vacuum is set up in the exhaust. This
         partial vacuum draws fuel into the crankcase.
         In many instances, this has resulted in bursting
         the crankcase or cylinders and pistons when
         the plant was started. To prevent this, the
         fuel line shut-off valve must be tightly closed
         whenever the plant is stopped, whether in flight
         or at the airship base.

(f) LaDel Electric Blower

The production schedule calls for a LaDel electric
blower to replace the gasoline powered blower, described
above, on airships K-99 and future. The only source of
power for this blower is the Lawrance auxiliary generator.
The auxiliary generator must be running at rated speed
before the electric blower may be used.

(5) Summary: Pressure Control System

    (a) Settings

        1. Forward Air Valve: Begins to open at 1.50 inches
          of water of air pressure in the forward ballonet
          as read on car manometer.

        2. Aft Air Valve: Begins to open at 2.00 inches of
          water of air pressure in the aft ballonet as
          read on car manometer.

        3. Gas Valve: Begins to open at 2-1/2-inches of
          water as read on gas manometer.

    (b) Control, Instruments & Auxiliaries Chart
        See Fig. XIII

    (c) Operation Chart
        See Fig. XIV

INSTRUMENTS, CONTROLS AUXILIARIES	LOCATION	PURPOSE
Air Scoop Adjustment	Port & Starboard of Frame 6.	To control air pressure in air chambers and ballonets.
Air Damper Contols	Pilot's Instrument Panel Fig. XI	To direct air to the forward or aft ballonet
Air Valve Controls	Pilot's Instrument Panel Fig. XI	To release air from the forward or aft ballonets and to close valve.
Manometers (3)	Pilot's Flight Panel Fig. XI	To indicate pressure of the gas in envelope and of the air in the two ballonets
Pressure Gage	Pilot's Instrument Panel Fig. XI	To check liquid gas pressure manometer
Auxiliary Blower	Cabin Deck, Frame 5, Fig. XII	To supply air pressure to ballonets when regular system becomes inadequate
Switch for Auxiliary Blower	Pilot's Instrument Board Fig. XI Also switch on engine	To shut off motor.
Gas Valve Controls	Pilot's Instrument Panel Fig. XI	To release gas manually and to close valve.
Air Sleeve	Ceiling Frame 6.	To blow air into gas in emergency
Rip Cords	Outside of Forward and Aft Doors	To deflate ship rapidly in emergency

Fig. XIII

Controls, Instruments and Auxiliaries Chart

OPERATION	CONDITION	NORMAL SETTING	REMARKS
Take-off	Air in both ballonets	Both dampers closed	Keep up ship inflation if necessary by opening dampers and by occasional blasts of propellers or by auxiliary blower
Climbing	Air being released from Fwd.Ballonet	Both dampers closed	Watch for excessive gas pressure. Stay below climbing rate of 1200 ft. per minute.
Flying near pressure height	Ballonets are fully deflated.Gas valves operate automatically to release gas if pressure height is exceeded.	Open both dampers and scoops.	Maintain full operating pressure in air system. Do not operate air valves manually. Check closing control of gas valves to make sure no gas is being lost. Watch the tell-tale lights.
Level Flight	Ship in trim. Air in both ballonets.	Open forward damper and regulate scoops to produce desired pressure	Consider air as regular ballast in determining effect of shift on trim.
Normal Descending	Air being normally replaced in forward ballonet	Open forward damper	Watch for too low pressure. Stay below descending rate of 600 ft. per minute.
Landing	Motors are throttled down.Pressure from regular system is inadequate	Start blower motor,open intake door, open both dampers.	See Page 44 for instructions to start blower motor.
Shifting Air		Use dampers & air valves as needed.	Consider air as regular ballast in determining effect of shift on trim.
Blowing air into gas	Excessive loss of gas	Untie sleeve which connects air to gas.	Blow only the minimum amount air necessary to maintain pressure.

Fig. XIV
Operation Chart – Pressure Control System

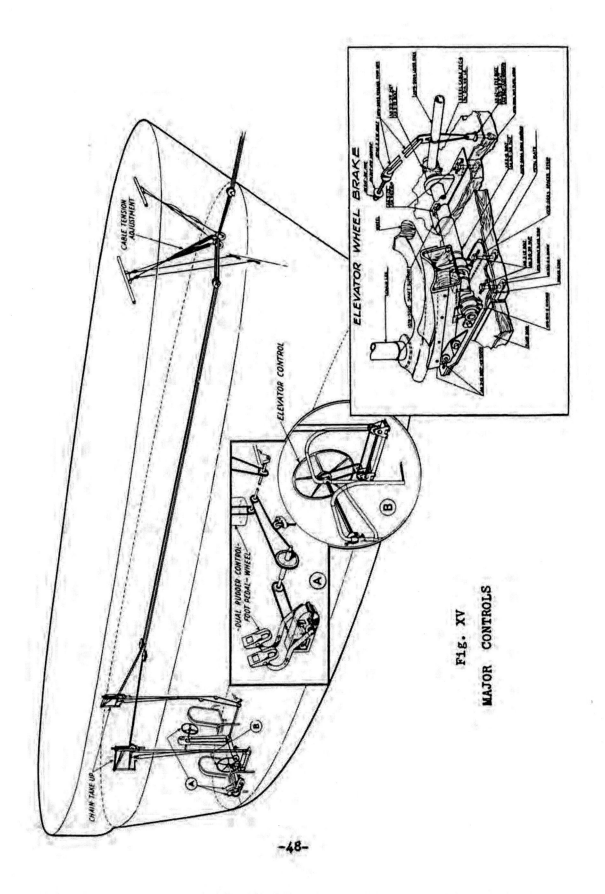

CABLE TENSION ADJUSTMENT

ELEVATOR WHEEL BRAKE

ELEVATOR CONTROL

DUAL RUDDER CONTROL FOOT PEDAL - WHEEL

A

B

CHAIN TAKE UP

Fig. XV

MAJOR CONTROLS

C. MAJOR CONTROLS

Occasional adjustments are required in the tension of the control lines of the major controls to compensate for slight changes in the shape of the envelope with variations of the pressure and of the loading. Tension varies particularly with the fullness of the aft ballonet, a large amount of air in this ballonet causing the cables to slacken.

An automatic tensioning device located in the aft portion of the car between frames 1 and 2 takes care of part of these variations. In addition, the tension can be adjusted from the pilot's compartment. The crank on the port side is for the elevator lines, and the one on the starboard side is for the rudder lines. The tension of the controls should be checked from time to time in flight. A check should always be made immediately after a heavy take-off, because of the added sagging of the envelope caused by the dynamic lift.

CAUTION: It is particularly important that the pilot check the controls and adjust the tension of the lines as required before take-off and before landing otherwise he may find himself without enough control in an emergency.

Occasional adjustments may also have to be made in flight.

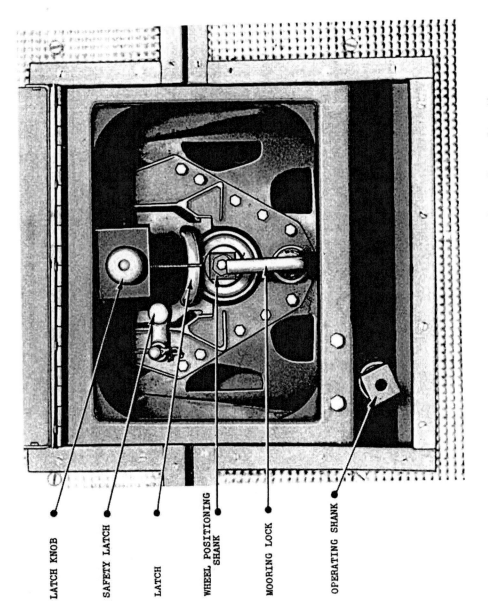

LATCH KNOB

SAFETY LATCH

LATCH

WHEEL POSITIONING SHANK

MOORING LOCK

OPERATING SHANK

Fig. XVI – Top of Landing Gear Strut

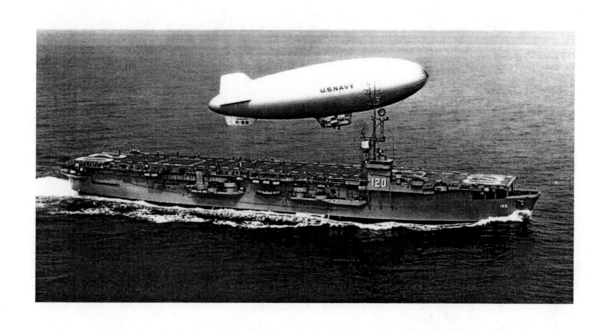

D. RETRACTABLE LANDING GEAR

  (1) To Drop Landing Gear

    (a) Open trap door giving access to landing gear
mechanism (car floor at frame 7).
    (b) See that mooring pin is up.
    (c) Place crank on top of operating shaft and crank
until top of strut is against the stop.
    (d) Make sure that the latch drops fully into place,
and lock it in place by means of the safety device.
    (e) Back off crank slightly to relieve pressure on
worm gear. Gear should now be ready for landing.

  (2) To Retract Landing Gear After Takeoff

    (a) Open access trap door and place crank on top of
strut shank.
    (b) Turn the shank until the guide fork on top of the
strut and the landing wheel are in a direct aft
position.
    (c) Drop the mooring pin and turn the crank slightly
to and fro until the pin drops into the slot in
the guide fork.
    (d) Unlock the safety device and raise the latch.
    (e) Place the crank on the operating shaft and turn
until the strut is fully retracted.
    (f) Raise the mooring pin.

  (3) To Lock Landing Gear at 90° To Axis Of Ship For
Operation On Mooring Mast

    (a) Turn strut in position by means of crank inserted
in positioning shank.
    (b) Push mooring lock in place.

E. HANDLING LINES

At take-off, the yaw lines are stowed in two compart-
ments in the bow of the car from where they can be released
by means of a control located at the left of the elevator
pilot. A drag rope can be released from a compartment in
the stern of the car by means of a control located on the
port side of frame 2.

PART III
POWER PLANT

GOODYEAR   K·AIRSHIP

========== III - POWER PLANT ==========

References:
1. Engine Manufacturer's Manual
2. BuAer Manual 14-101 to 14-506

A. ENGINES

    (1) General Characteristics

        (a) K-3 thru K-8 :   R-975-28 Wright Aero.

             Take-off rating: 450 H.P. at 2250 r.p.m. at sea level.

             Normal rating: 420 H.P. at 2200 r.p.m. at sea level.

             Gear Ratio: Direct Drive

             Fuel: Aviation grade, 91 octane, AN Spec. AN-F-26

             Oil: W.A.C. Spec. No. 5815

        (b) From K-9 on: R 1340 - AN Pratt & Whitney Wasp

             Normal Rating: 425 H.P. at 1775 r.p.m. at sea level

             Gear Ratio: 3:2

             Fuel: AN Spec. No. AN-VV-O-446a

    (2) Starting

        The starters are of the hand electric inertia type.

In starting, proceed as follows:

(a) In cold weather plug in oil tank electric heater until

    tank feels warm to the hand.

(b) Turn the engines over four or five revolutions by pull-

    ing the propeller through by hand.

(c) Set carburetor heat control in "cold" position.

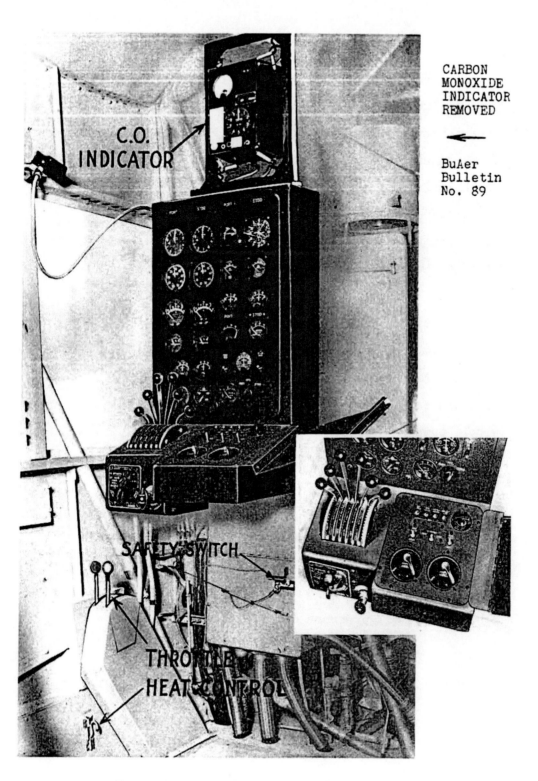

CARBON
MONOXIDE
INDICATOR
REMOVED

←

BuAer
Bulletin
No. 89

C.O.
INDICATOR

SAFETY SWITCH

THROTTLE
HEAT CONTROL

Fig. XVIII Mechanic's Panel

(d) Set carburetor mixture to "rich."

(e) Turn on fuel supply.

(f) Open throttle to the position corresponding to 600 RPM.

(g) Turn primer pump handle in the direction of the engine which it is desired to start, (to the right for the starboard engine, to the left for the port engine), give from 2 to 5 strokes of the pump after the priming line has been filled, and reset handle to neutral position.

(h) Turn ignition switch to "Both On."

(i) Make certain that main battery switch is closed.

(j) Turn generator switch on.

(k) Maintain about 3 lbs./sq.in. fuel pressure with the wobble pump.

(l) Select motor to be started by means of selector switch.

(m) Push starter switch to "on" position, wait about 30 seconds until the whine of the starter indicates that it is running full speed and pull switch to "mesh."

(n) Repeat, if necessary, until engine starts.

CAUTION: If oil pressure does not come up to normal in 30 seconds, stop engines and investigate.

(3) <u>Warming Up</u>

    (a) Set carburetor heat control to full hot.

    (b) Set the throttle for a speed of about 600 RPM.

    (c) After about one minute raise the speed to about 1000 RPM.

    CAUTION: <u>Do not attempt to operate engines over 1000 RPM until the oil-in temperature has exceeded 100°F. (38°C) and do not exceed 1400 RPM for continued operation on the ground under any condition.</u>

                <u>Do not idle engines at speeds causing bad vibrations. Critical vibrations occur between 750 to 900 RPM.</u>

(4) <u>Ground Test</u>

    Check RPM when operating on one or two magnetos. The drop in RPM when shifting from both magnetos to either of them should not exceed 100 RPM, and 40 RPM when shifting from one magneto to the other. Check oil pressure, oil temperature, fuel pressure and battery charging rate.

(5) <u>Take Off</u>

    (a) Use both service tanks.

    (b) Open valve in cross connecting fuel line between the two engine fuel pumps.

    (c) Check oil temperature.

    (d) Cylinder head temperature should preferably not exceed 260° C. at the time of take off.

    (e) Set mixture control to "rich."

    (f) Return preheat valve to full cold as throttles are opened.

(g) Open throttle gradually (3 to 5 seconds desirable) being careful not to exceed limiting manifold pressure.

(6) <u>Cruising</u>   (Reference Buaer Manual 14-206)

    (a) Do not exceed operating limits.

    (b) Wait until motors have cooled down before leaning carburetor.

    (c) Do not lean carburetor beyond 10 RPM drop of speed.

CAUTION: <u>It must be kept in mind that while a lean mixture increases fuel economy, it also increases heating of the engine. Leaning is only permissible at reduced power output. See Engine Operator's Handbook for full discussion of the matter of carburetor setting.</u>

(7) <u>Single Engine Operation</u>

Whenever it is found necessary to operate on only one engine, stop other engine as directed below and leave mixture control on "Idle Cut-Off" position with closed throttle. This setting insures that the wind-milling of the engine will draw minimum of fuel into the cylinder.

(8) <u>Stopping</u>

    (a) Move mixture control to "Idle Cut-Off" position.

    (b) When the engines have stopped, turn all ignition switches to "Off" position.

    (c) In emergency, the motors can be stopped from the pilot instrument panel by means of two ignition grounding switches.

CAUTION: If engines are hot, run them at idling
speed until cylinder temperature has
dropped below 400 F. (220 C.) before
stopping.

(9) Operating Limits and Charts

    (a) Operating Limits for Wright Engine
       (K-3 thru K-8 Airships). See page 59.

    (b) Operating Limits for Pratt-Whitney Engines
       (K-9 and Subsequent Airships). See page 60

    (c) Power Output of Wright Engine at Sea Level and
       1500 Ft. Altitude. See pages 61 and 62

    (d) Power Output of Pratt-Whitney Engines at Sea
       Level and 1500 ft. Altitude. See pages 63 & 64

    (e) Fuel Consumption of Wright Engine.
       See page 65

    (f) Fuel Consumption of Pratt-Whitney Engines.
       See page 66

    (g) Most Economical Air Speed. See page 67.

    (h) Mechanic's Check Chart for Pratt-Whitney
       Engines. See page 68.

OPERATING LIMITS FOR WRIGHT WHIRLWIND R-975-28

K-3 to K-8 Airships

Minimum Oil Inlet Temperature for Take-Off.....................	104°F. or 40°C.
Desired Oil Temperature..........	140°F. or 60°C.
Maximum Inlet Temperature.......	190°F. or 88°C.
Maximum Cylinder Temperature for Take-Off.....................	500°F. or 260°C.
Maximum Cylinder Temperature (Cruising).....................	450°F. or 230°C.
Desired Cylinder Temperature...	325°F. or 163°C.
Minimum Oil Pressure (Idling).....................	10 lbs./sq.in.
Minimum Oil Pressure (Cruising).....................	50 lbs./sq.in.
Desired Oil Pressure...........	60-80 lbs./sq.in.
Fuel Pressure.....................	2.5-3.5 lbs./sq.in.

OPERATING LIMITS FOR PRATT & WHITNEY R-1340 WASP ENGINE

For K-9 and Future

Minimum Oil Inlet Temperature
for Take-off .... 40° C.

Desired Oil Inlet Temperature .... 60° C. - 75° C.

Maximum Oil Inlet Temperature .... 85° C.

Maximum Cylinder Temperature
-1 to 1-1/2 Min.Climb .... Head 260° C.
                                              Base 168° C.

Maximum Cylinder Temperature
-Continuous Cruising .... Head 232° C.
                                              Base 93° C. 121° C.

Minimum Oil Pressure
(At idling speeds) .... 10 lbs./sq.in.

Minimum at 1000 R.P.M. .... 40 lbs./sq.in.

Minimum at 1400 R.P.M. .... 50 lbs./sq.in.

Desired Oil Pressure at and above
1400 R.P.M. .... 70-90 lbs./sq.in.

For Setting:
1400 R.P.M., 65°C. Oil-in, using 1100 Oil .. 80 lbs./sq.in.

Minimum Fuel Pressure (400 RPM or less) .... 2 lbs./sq.in.

Minimum Fuel Pressure
(1000 RPM or above) .... 4 lbs./sq.in.

Desired Fuel Pressure
(1000 RPM or above) .... 5 lbs.sq.in.

Maximum Fuel Pressure
(1000 RPM or above) .... 6 lbs./sq.in.

Desired Carburetor Air Intake Temperature.
  Note: Take-off - Return controls to
        "Full Cold" as throttles are opened.

    Idling .... 50° C.

    Cruising: 1400 RPM or less .... 50° C.
              Above 1400 RPM with stabilized
              operating conditions .... 38° C.

-60-

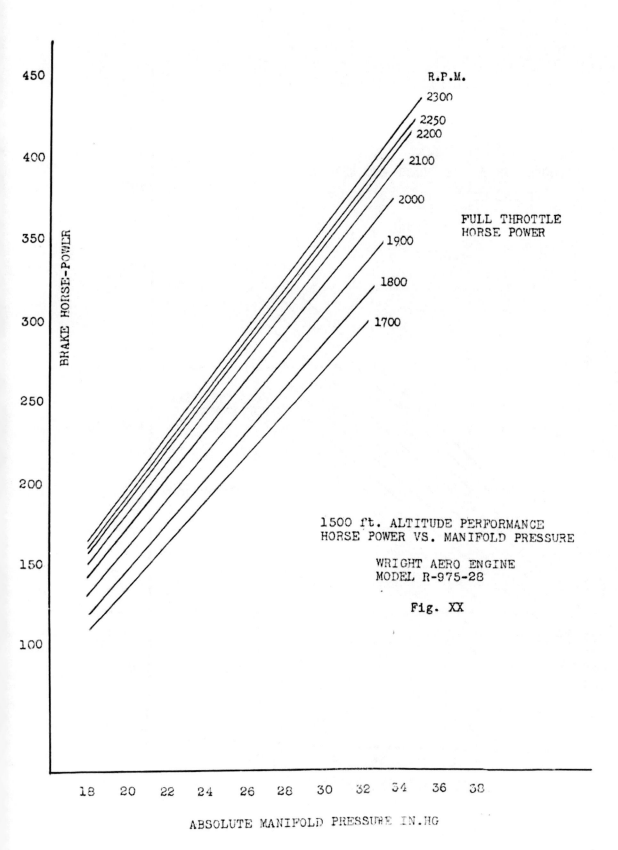

R.P.M.

2300
2250
2200
2100
2000
1900
1800
1700

FULL THROTTLE
HORSE POWER

1500 ft. ALTITUDE PERFORMANCE
HORSE POWER VS. MANIFOLD PRESSURE

WRIGHT AERO ENGINE
MODEL R-975-28

Fig. XX

BRAKE HORSE-POWER

ABSOLUTE MANIFOLD PRESSURE IN.HG

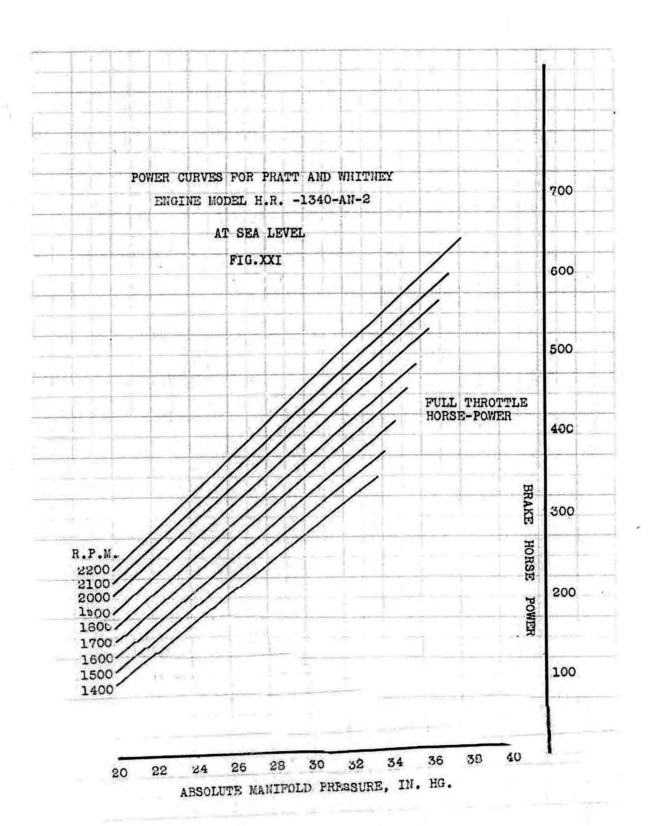

POWER CURVES FOR PRATT AND WHITNEY
ENGINE MODEL H.R. -1340-AN-2
AT SEA LEVEL
FIG.XXI

FULL THROTTLE
HORSE-POWER

R.P.M.
2200
2100
2000
1900
1800
1700
1600
1500
1400

BRAKE HORSE POWER

700
600
500
400
300
200
100

20   22   24   26   28   30   32   34   36   38   40

ABSOLUTE MANIFOLD PRESSURE, IN. HG.

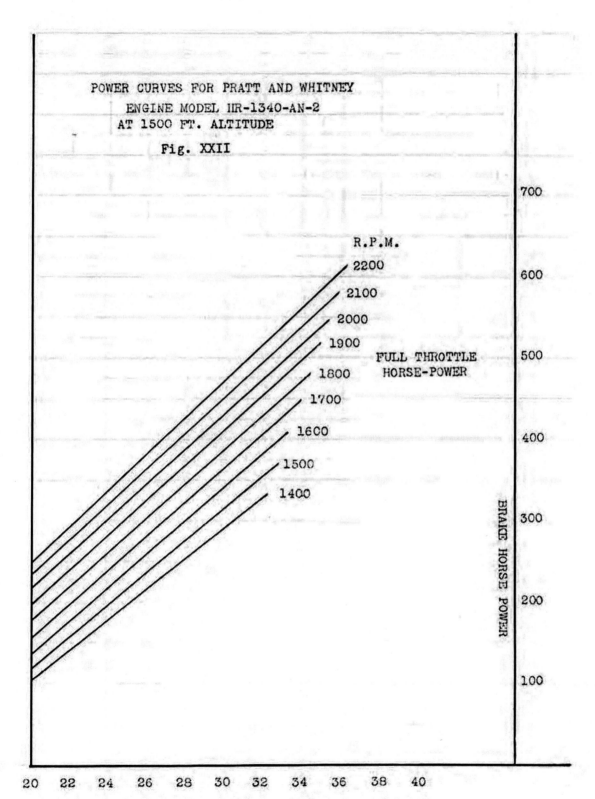

POWER CURVES FOR PRATT AND WHITNEY
ENGINE MODEL IIR-1340-AN-2
AT 1500 FT. ALTITUDE

Fig. XXII

R.P.M.
2200
2100
2000
1900
1800
1700
1600
1500
1400

FULL THROTTLE
HORSE-POWER

BRAKE HORSE POWER

700
600
500
400
300
200
100

20 22 24 26 28 30 32 34 36 38 40

ABSOLUTE MANIFOLD PRESSURE, IN.HG.

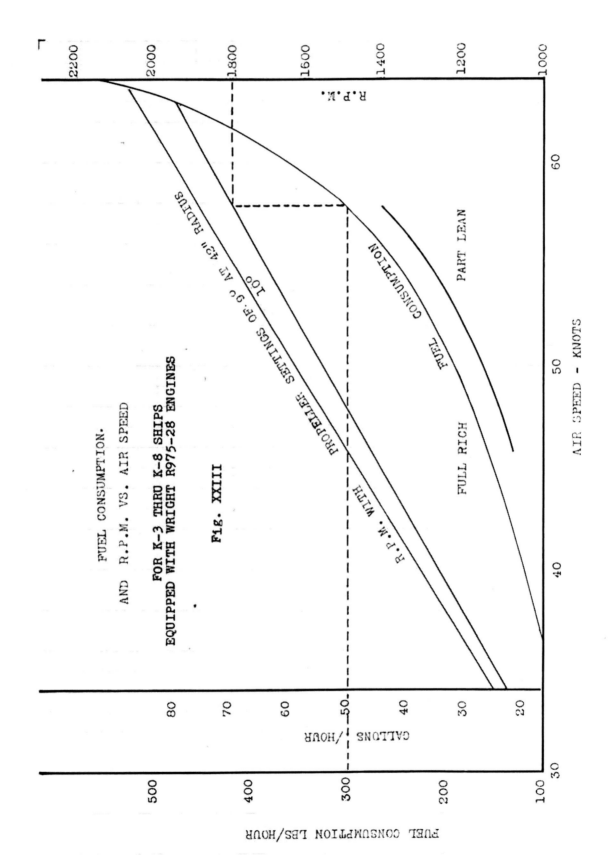

FUEL CONSUMPTION.
AND R.P.M. VS. AIR SPEED
FOR K-3 THRU K-8 SHIPS
EQUIPPED WITH WRIGHT R975-28 ENGINES

Fig. XXIII

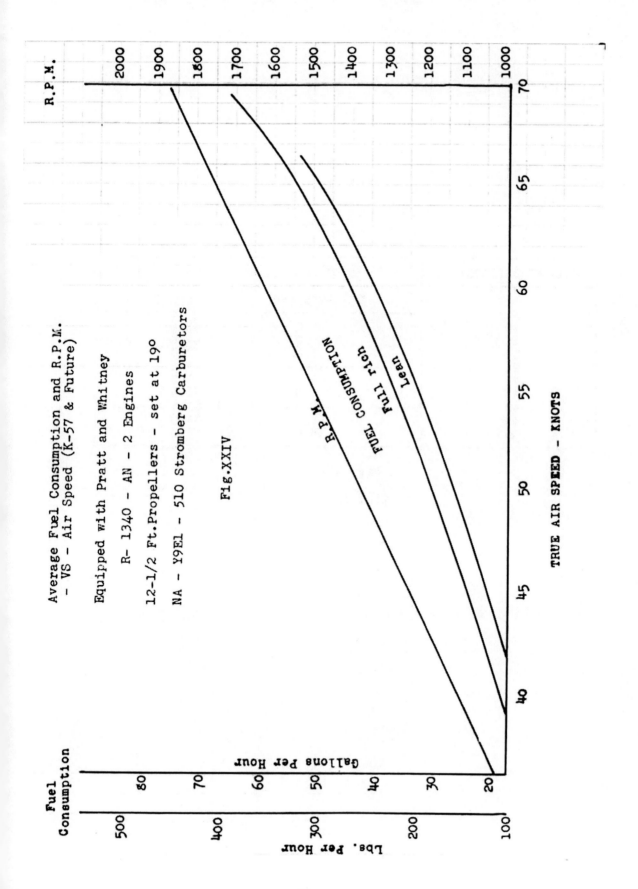

Average Fuel Consumption and R.P.M.
- VS - Air Speed (K-57 & Future)

Equipped with Pratt and Whitney

R- 1340 - AN - 2 Engines

12-1/2 Ft.Propellers - set at 19°

NA - Y9E1 - 510 Stromberg Carburetors

Fig.XXIV

R.P.M.

FUEL CONSUMPTION

Full rich

Lean

TRUE AIR SPEED - KNOTS

R.P.M.

Fuel Consumption

Gallons Per Hour

Lbs. Per Hour

HEAD WIND VELOCITY, KNOTS	MOST ECONOMICAL AIR SPEED, KNOTS	
	K-3 thru K-8	K-9 and Future
10	46.0	42.0
15	46.0	42.0
20	46.0	42.0
25	46.0	43.5
30	49.0	50.0
35	51.5	56.5
40	56.0	62.5
45	58.0	64.0
50	58.0	64.0

Fig. XXV

Economical Air Speeds

Operating Condition	Engine R.P.M.	Mixture Control	Carburetor Air Temp.	Oil Inlet Temp.	Cyl. Head Temp.	Oil Pressure lbs./in^2	REMARKS
Start	Set Throttle for 600 R.P.M.	FULL RICH	FULL COLD			Must Show in 30 Sec.	In cold weather heat oil in out-rigger tanks by means of electrical units.
Warm Up	500-600 For 1 Min. After 1000 After (2)	FULL RICH	FULL HOT			50 Minimum	Do not exceed 1400 r.p.m. for continual operation.
Ground Test	1400	FULL RICH	32°C.	37.8°C. Minimum	204°C.	70-90	Drop in R.P.M. when shifting from one magneto to the other should not exceed 40.
Take-Off	1800 Max.	FULL RICH	32°C.	60-64°C.	233°C.	70-90	Max. rating 600 H.P. at 2250 R.P.M.
Cruising Desired	1300	PART LEAN	32°C.	60-64°C.	204°C. or Less Desired	70-90	Do not lean carburetor beyond 10 R.P.M. drop of speed.
Stopping	400-500	FULL LEAN					Idle engine until cylinder temperature has dropped below 220°C. before stopping.

1. With propeller setting of 23° at 42" radius do not fly ship faster than 67 knots.

2. Do not operate engines at speeds causing bed vibrations. Maximum vibrations occur between 650 to 900 r.p.m.

Fig.XXVI Mechanic's Check Chart

Pratt and Whitney R1340 - AN2 Wasp Engine

B. FUEL SYSTEM

The fuel system of the K-airship is designed to make possible the shifting of fuel for the purpose of trimming the ship without interference with the normal feed of the engine. This is accomplished by carrying the bulk of the fuel in two banks of storage tanks, a forward and an aft bank, and by feeding the engines from two service tanks which can be isolated from the rest of the system. The service tanks can be filled from either bank of storage tanks without interruption to the feed of the engines.

The system can be filled through an outside connection or through an inside connection by means of the transfer pump.

Provisions are made for dumping fuel from aft storage tanks and for the release of two slip tanks located under the floor of the cabin, for the transfer of fuel from the slip tanks to the rest of the system and for the proper filtering of the fuel.

CAUTION: 1. At take-off, always open valve in cross-connecting fuel line to insure against a fuel pump failure.

2. Make certain that there is ample fuel in the service tanks at all times during flight.

3. Do not dump fuel when either of the auxiliary engines is running.

4. Clean the four fuel strainers after every
   120 hours flying time, and oftener, if
   necessary. The strainers should be cleaned
   immediately when irregular operation of either
   engine develops.

   For the location of the strainers and
   instructions <u>for cleaning them in flight,</u>
   see Fig. XXVII on the following page.

5. Make certain that pressure in fuel system does
   not exceed 25 lbs. per sq.in. when filling
   from external pump.

6. Do not feed engines from a tank containing
   less than 12 gallons of fuel as the outlet
   is nearly uncovered with this amount of fuel
   still in the tank, and with the ship at a
   30° angle of pitch.

The various operations which can be performed with
the system, together with the proper settings of the valves,
are described in Figures XXVIII-a thru XXVIII-j for K-3
thru K-10 airships, and in Figures XXIX-a thru XXIX-j for
K-11 and future.

C. <u>RECOMMENDED CARBURETOR ADJUSTMENT</u>

   (a) Run engine at 400 RPM.
   (b) Cylinder head temperature should be normal.
   (c) Have good plugs in engine.
   (d) Have mixture control FULL RICH.
   (e) Note RPM.
   (f) Rapidly move mixture control from FULL RICH to
       IDLE CUT OFF position. Catch the engine
       before it stalls.
   (g) Note RPM.
       1. If large gain in RPM - Carburetor is set too
          rich.
       2. If loss in RPM - Carburetor is set too lean.
       3. Desired - gain of from 0 to 10 RPM.

The desired setting is the RICH BEST POWER setting
for the carburetor at the idle speed of the engine.

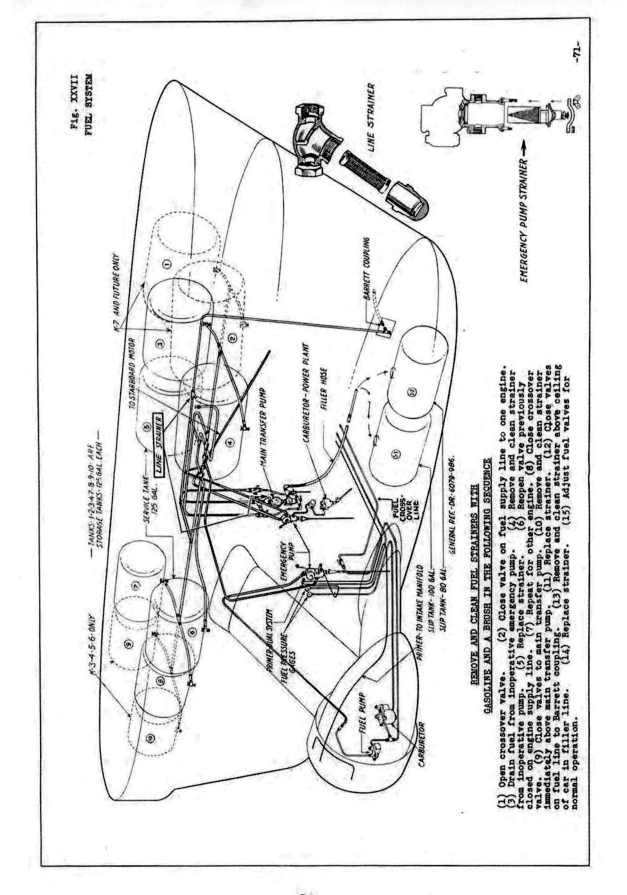

Fig. XXVII
FUEL SYSTEM

LINE STRAINER

EMERGENCY PUMP STRAINER →

- TANKS: 1-2-3-4-7-8-9-10-ARE -
STORAGE TANKS: 125 GAL. EACH -

K-7 AND FUTURE ONLY

TO STARBOARD MOTOR

BARRETT COUPLING

SERVICE TANK
125 GAL.

LINE STRAINER

MAIN TRANSFER PUMP

CARBURETOR-POWER PLANT

FILLER HOSE

K-3-4-5-6- ONLY

EMERGENCY PUMP

FUEL PRESSURE GAGES

PRIMER FUEL SYSTEM

PRIMER-TO INTAKE MANIFOLD

SLIP TANK-100 GAL.

SLIP TANK-80 GAL.

FUEL CROSS-OVER LINE

GENERAL REF.-DR.6079-986.

FUEL PUMP

CARBURETOR

REMOVE AND CLEAN FUEL STRAINERS WITH
GASOLINE AND A BRUSH IN THE FOLLOWING SEQUENCE

(1) Open crossover valve.   (2) Close valve on fuel supply line to one engine.
(3) Drain fuel from inoperative emergency pump.   (4) Remove and clean strainer
from inoperative pump.   (5) Replace strainer.   (6) Reopen valve previously
closed on engine supply line.   (7) Repeat for other engine. (8) Close crossover
valve.   (9) Close valves to main transfer pump.   (10) Remove and clean strainer
immediately above main transfer pump.   (11) Replace strainer.   (12) Close valves
on fuel line to Barrett coupling.   (13) Remove and clean strainer above ceiling
of car in filler line.   (14) Replace strainer.   (15) Adjust fuel valves for
normal operation.

-71-

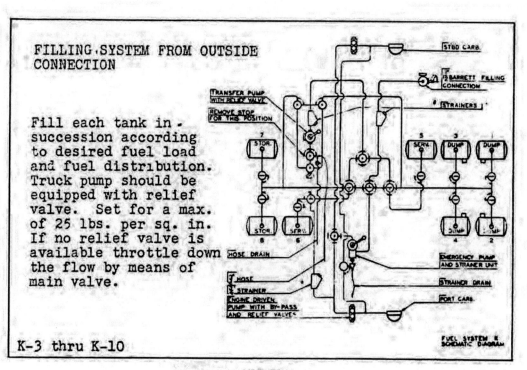

FILLING SYSTEM FROM OUTSIDE CONNECTION

Fill each tank in succession according to desired fuel load and fuel distribution. Truck pump should be equipped with relief valve. Set for a max. of 25 lbs. per sq. in. If no relief valve is available throttle down the flow by means of main valve.

K-3 thru K-10

Fig. XXVIII-a

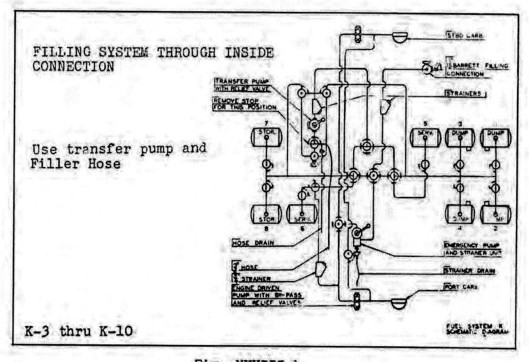

FILLING SYSTEM THROUGH INSIDE CONNECTION

Use transfer pump and Filler Hose

K-3 thru K-10

Fig. XXVIII-b

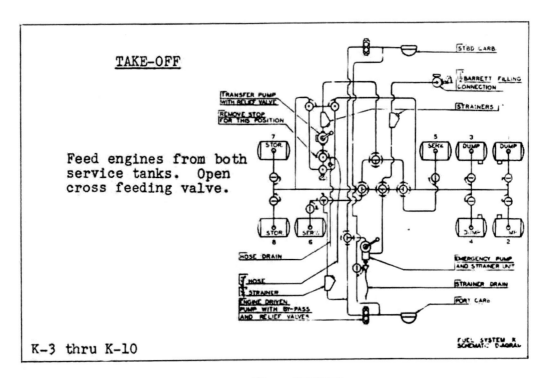

TAKE-OFF

Feed engines from both service tanks. Open cross feeding valve.

K-3 thru K-10

Fig. XXVIII-c

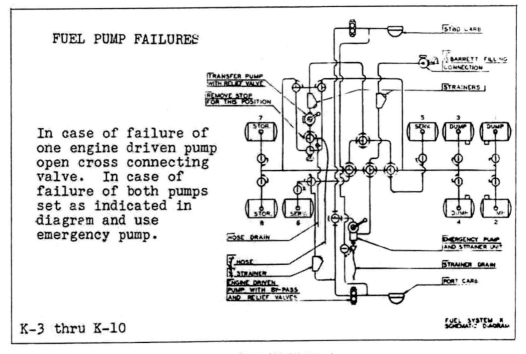

FUEL PUMP FAILURES

In case of failure of one engine driven pump open cross connecting valve. In case of failure of both pumps set as indicated in diagram and use emergency pump.

K-3 thru K-10

Fig. XXVIII-d

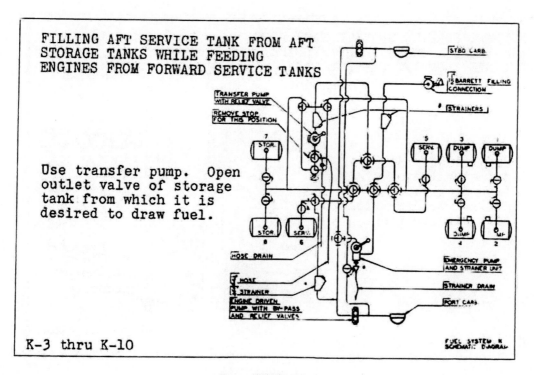

FILLING AFT SERVICE TANK FROM AFT
STORAGE TANKS WHILE FEEDING
ENGINES FROM FORWARD SERVICE TANKS

Use transfer pump. Open
outlet valve of storage
tank from which it is
desired to draw fuel.

K-3 thru K-10

Fig. XXVIII-e

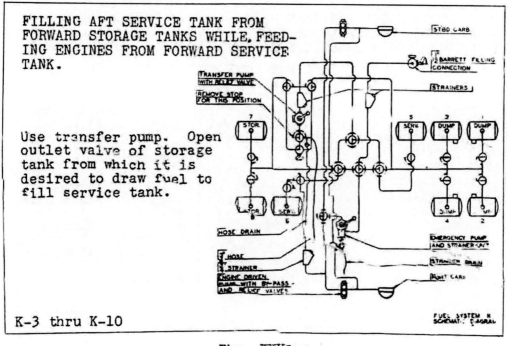

FILLING AFT SERVICE TANK FROM
FORWARD STORAGE TANKS WHILE FEED-
ING ENGINES FROM FORWARD SERVICE
TANK.

Use transfer pump. Open
outlet valve of storage
tank from which it is
desired to draw fuel to
fill service tank.

K-3 thru K-10

Fig. XXVIII-f

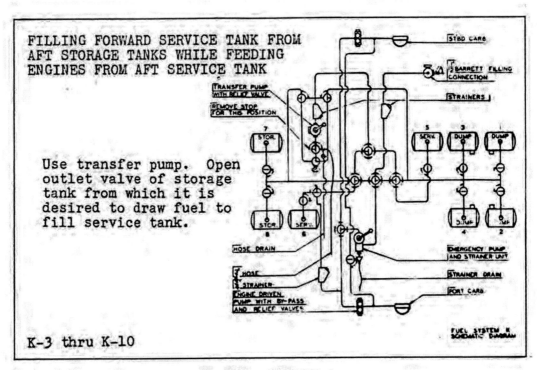

FILLING FORWARD SERVICE TANK FROM
AFT STORAGE TANKS WHILE FEEDING
ENGINES FROM AFT SERVICE TANK

Use transfer pump. Open
outlet valve of storage
tank from which it is
desired to draw fuel to
fill service tank.

K-3 thru K-10

Fig. XXVIII-g

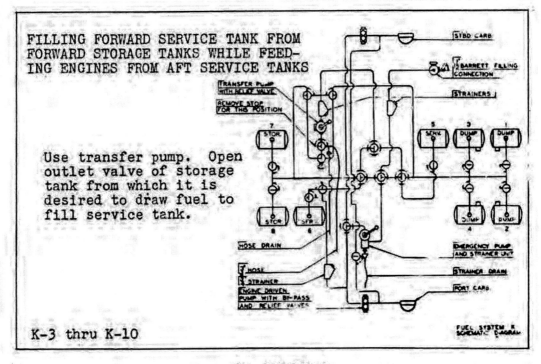

FILLING FORWARD SERVICE TANK FROM
FORWARD STORAGE TANKS WHILE FEED-
ING ENGINES FROM AFT SERVICE TANKS

Use transfer pump. Open
outlet valve of storage
tank from which it is
desired to draw fuel to
fill service tank.

K-3 thru K-10

Fig.XXVIII-h

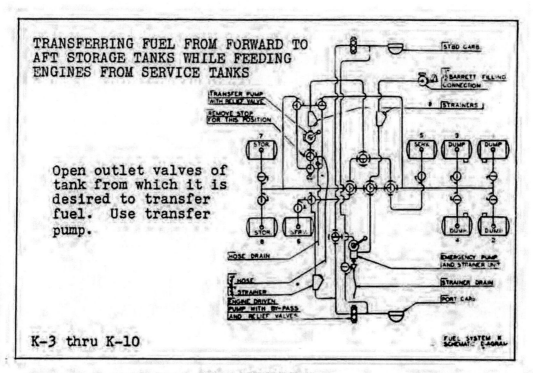

Fig. XXVIII-i

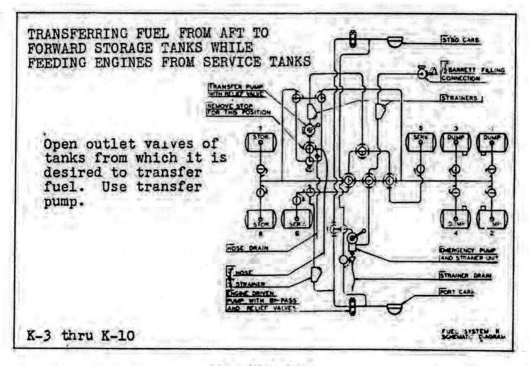

Fig. XXVIII-j

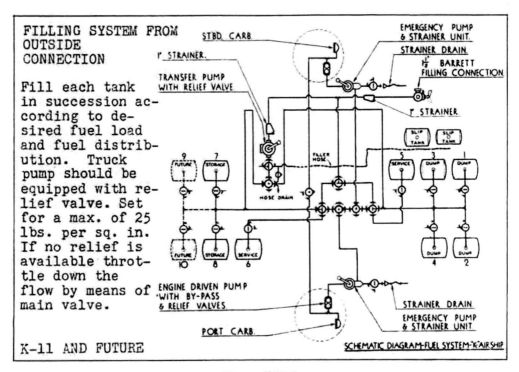

FILLING SYSTEM FROM OUTSIDE CONNECTION

Fill each tank in succession according to desired fuel load and fuel distribution. Truck pump should be equipped with relief valve. Set for a max. of 25 lbs. per sq. in. If no relief is available throttle down the flow by means of main valve.

K-11 AND FUTURE

Fig. XXIX-a

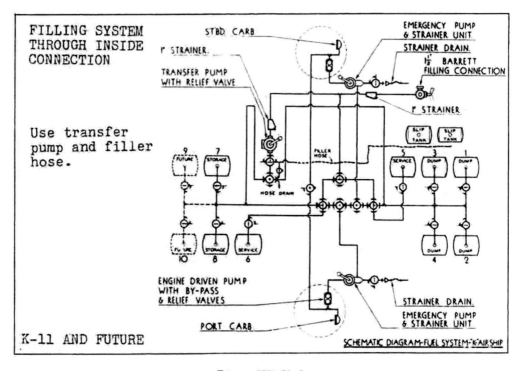

FILLING SYSTEM THROUGH INSIDE CONNECTION

Use transfer pump and filler hose.

K-11 AND FUTURE

Fig. XXIX-b

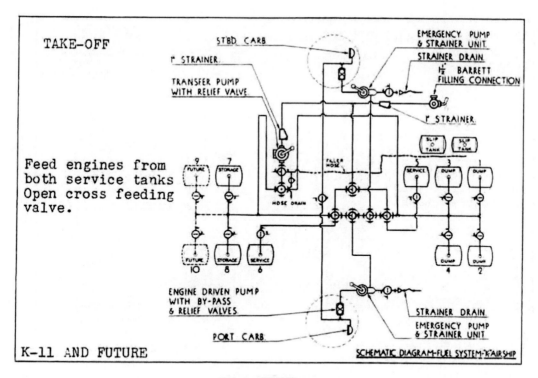

Fig. XXIX-c

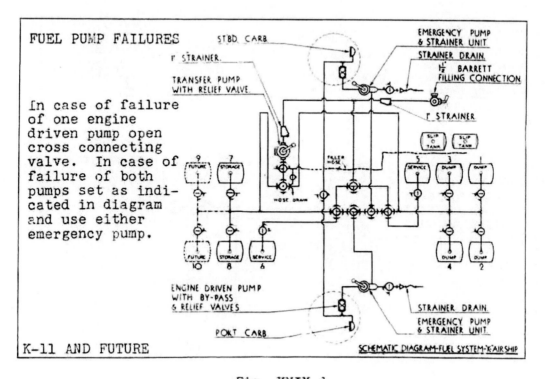

Fig. XXIX-d

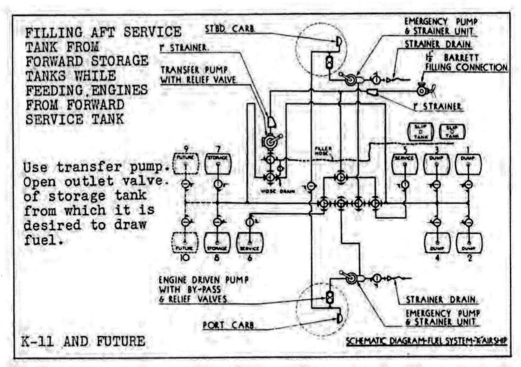

Fig. XXIX-e

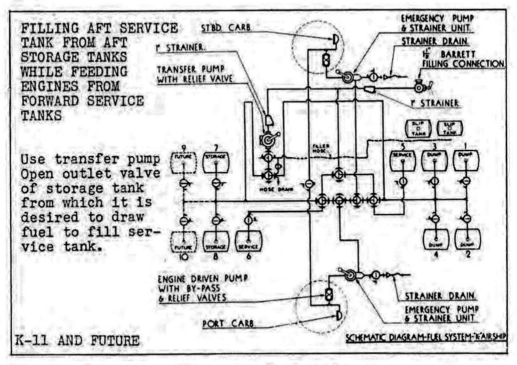

Fig. XXIX-f

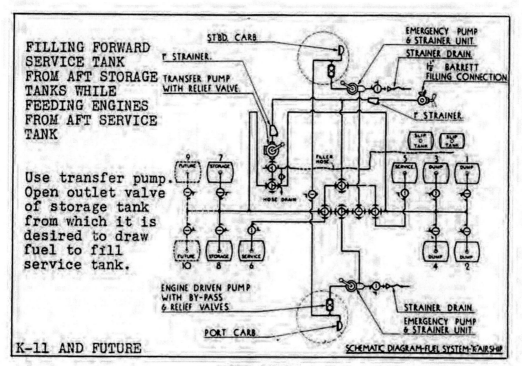

Fig. XXIX-g

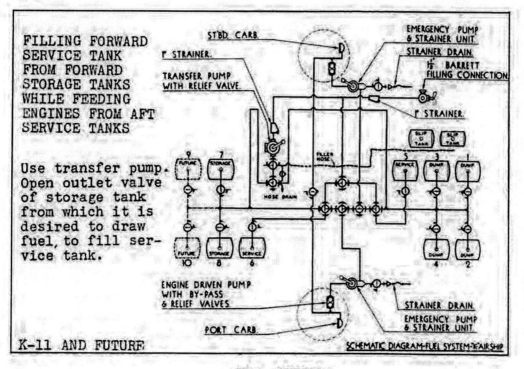

Fig. XXIX-h

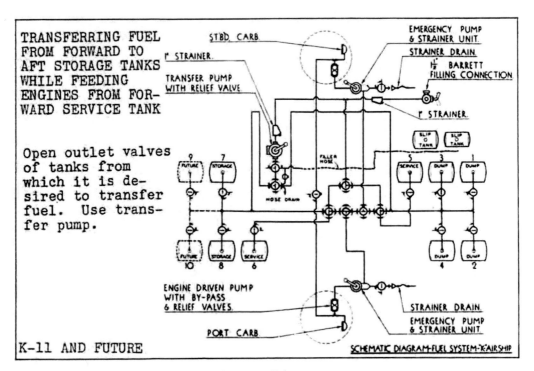

Fig. XXIX-i

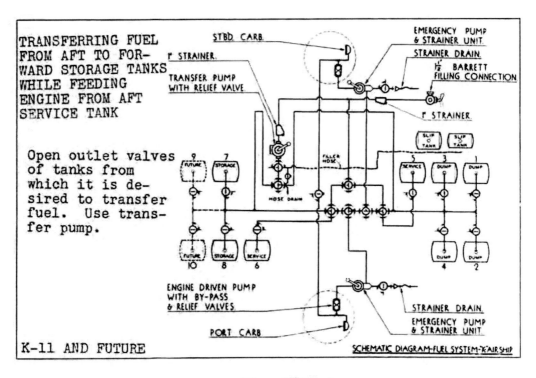

Fig. XXIX-j

D. OIL SYSTEM

The oil system for K-3 thru K-74 includes a 30-gallon
oil storage tank below the deck of the car, and two
14-gallon oil service tanks, one in each engine nacelle,
and a transfer pump with necessary fittings.

In K-75 and future, the oil storage tank, transfer
pump and fittings are removed and the oil service tanks in
the nacelles are enlarged to the 26-gallon size.

The oil is cooled by a radiator which is located in
the nacelle for the K-3 thru K-8 airships, and which is
suspended from the lower outriggers for the K-9 and sub-
sequent ships.

The service tanks are equipped with electrical heating
units to heat the oil in cold weather.

The amount of oil in the service tanks is read on two
oil gages located on the mechanic's panel. The amount of
oil in the storage tanks is read directly on the tank
through a trap door in the deck of the car.

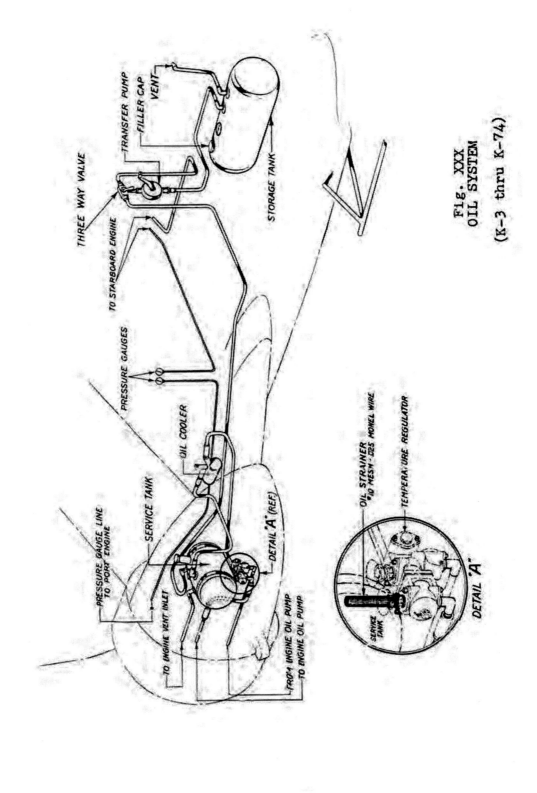

Fig. XXX
OIL SYSTEM
(K-3 thru K-74)

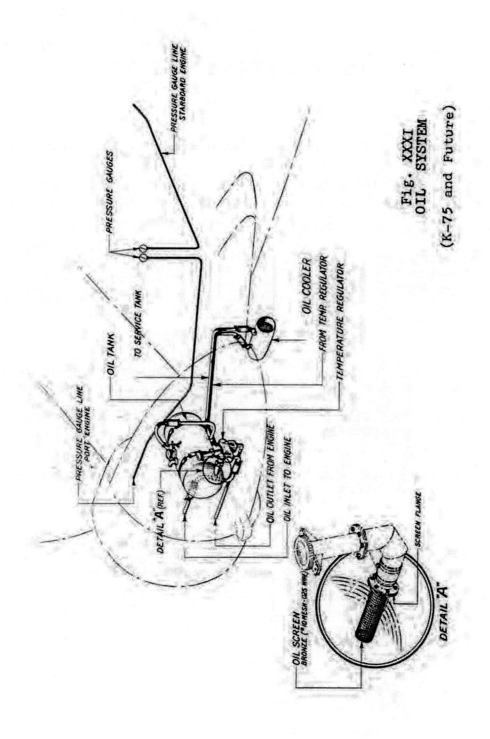

PRESSURE GAUGE LINE STARBOARD ENGINE

PRESSURE GAUGES

TO SERVICE TANK

OIL TANK

PRESSURE GAUGE LINE PORT ENGINE

OIL COOLER

FROM TEMP REGULATOR

TEMPERATURE REGULATOR

OIL OUTLET FROM ENGINE

OIL INLET TO ENGINE

DETAIL "A" (REF)

SCREEN FLANGE

OIL SCREEN BRONZE ("40-MESH-.125 WW)

DETAIL "A"

Fig. XXXI
OIL SYSTEM
(K-75 and Future)

-84-

SUMMARY OF OPERATION OF OIL SYSTEM

OPERATIONS	REMARKS
Filling system with oil. (K-3 thru K-74)	Fill storage tank through connection inside car and fill service tanks by means of transfer pump.
Filling service tank from storage tank. (K-3 thru K-74)	Use transfer pump.
Cleaning oil filter. (K-3 thru K-8)	Turn knob on top of filter one full revolution every ten (10) hours operation.
Regulating cooling. (K-3 thru K-8)	Adjust opening of scoops by means of control on mechanic's stand.
Heating oil before starting engines. (All ships)	Plug in electrical heating unit.
Filling system with oil. (K-75 and Future)	Fill each 26-gallon service tank thru filler neck which extends thru inboard forward nacelle at end of catwalk.
Cleaning oil filter. (K-9 and Future)	Remove and clean oil filters at each major overhaul, interim overhaul, or oftener if conditions are unfavorable. See Oil System diagram for location of filters.

================== IV.   ELECTRICAL SYSTEM ==================

References:

1. Equipment Manufacturer's Manuals
2. BuAer Manual 10-201 to 10-205.

A. GENERAL DESCRIPTION

The electrical system comprises an 800-cycle, 120-volt AC supply, and a 24-volt DC supply. The DC supply operates in connection with two 12-volt storage batteries. The batteries are connected in series.

The system as a whole includes three separate power producers, namely, the port generator, starboard generator, and Lawrance auxiliary power plant.

CAPACITY IN AMPERES

PRODUCERS	110-Volt, 800-Cycles or	24-Volt DC
Port Generator	7-9	25
Starboard Generator	7-9	25

120-Volt, 800-Cycles

Auxiliary Generator	41.7	167 Amp. @ 30 Volts.

The DC output of any or all generators can be thrown on the line to charge the battery and to supply the DC load.

B. DISTRIBUTION

        The electrical system is distributed from two panels, the auxiliary panel on the starboard side of the car between frames 5 and 6, and the mechanic's main panel. All the AC system and the DC output of the auxiliary generator come to the auxiliary panel. The DC output of the port and starboard generators come to the mechanic's panel. See Fig. XVIII and Fig. XXXIII.

NOTE: K-3 thru K-29 - as stated below.
            K-30 & Future - see installation of Lawrance
                    auxiliary generator.

        The auxiliary panel carries a selector switch to connect the AC loads to the generators in various combinations in accordance with the following table which is reproduced on the panel:

SWITCH POSITION	1	2	3	4
Starboard Generator	Radio	Off	Cook	Cook
	Cook	Radio	Off	Radio
	Off	Cook	Radio	Off

        The cooking loads consist of a roasterette, a hot plate and a percolator. A cooking panel equipped with a selector switch makes it impossible to connect more than one load at a time.

        The battery can be disconnected from the system by means of a safety switch located in the main junction box under the mechanic's panel and controlled both from the pilot's instrument panel and from the mechanic's stand.

FIG. XXXIII - AUXILIARY PANEL

The generator switches of K-11 ships and future are equipped with the thermal overload devices which operate when the normal load is exceeded.

To reset a generator switch after it has tripped open, wait until the overload device has cooled, and close the switch again.

C. CONTROL BOXES AND CUTOUTS

There is a control box and a cutout for each generator. The control boxes are the carbon pile type. See Fig. XXXIV.

(1) Carbon Pile Regulator

No adjustment or repairs should be attempted in flight on the carbon pile regulator.

(2) Service Troubles

(a) If the DC voltage output is erratic or low, check all connections to be sure they are clean and tight, and examine voltage regulator plug in connections for corrosion or poor contact. Spread plug in prongs, if necessary, to insure contact. If the regular contacts are dirty or pitted, they should be cleaned as instructed under "CONTROL BOX INSPECTION."

(b) If at any time the voltmeter shows a reversal of polarity by reading off scale in the wrong direction, or if the voltage reading is not more than 4 or 5 volts, the

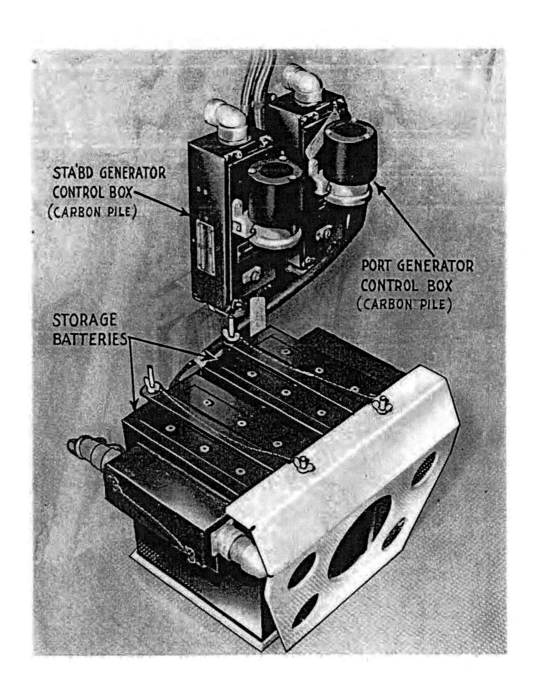

STA'BD GENERATOR
CONTROL BOX
(CARBON PILE)

PORT GENERATOR
CONTROL BOX
(CARBON PILE)

STORAGE
BATTERIES

FIG. XXXIV GENERATOR CONTROL
BOX AND BATTERY INSTALLATION

indications are that either the DC field has been inadver-
tently "flashed" in the wrong direction, or that the
generator is operating on residual magnetism only. To
"flash" the field, remove the (A+) lead from the generator
and momentarily close the generator cutout contacts, making
certain that the external connections to the battery are
correctly connected with regard to polarity.

(c) If the ammeter indicates zero charging current
when the generator voltage is above 13.5 or 26.8 volts for
12 or 24-volt systems respectively, check the operation of
the generator cutout contacts. If the contacts are open,
the unit is out of adjustment and should be reset in accordance with manufacturer's cutout instructions. If the contacts
are closed, check the charge on the battery, since the charging current drops down to a low value when operating with a
fully charged battery resulting in little or no ammeter
indication.

(d) If the AC voltage output is below the normal 120
volts (=5%), check the DC voltage output and readjust to
proper value as instructed under "CONTROL BOX INSPECTION."

Switches (Cont.)	Location
Navigation lights, running lights, instruments light, galley light.	Mechanic's panel.

(2) Automatic Controls

Port and starboard generator's control box.	Back of mechanic's main junction.
Port and Starboard cutouts.	Main junction box.
Aux. generator control box.	Aft of auxiliary pane. (Location changed K-30 & Fut.)
Aux. generator cutout.	Aux. panel junction box. (Aux.panel K-30 & Future).
Blinker	Top of mechanic's stand.

(3) Instruments

3 A.C. Ammeters and 3 A.C. voltmeters for port, starboard and aux. generators.	Auxiliary panel. Changed K-30 & future. (No A.C. Ammeter (One A.C. Voltmeter
1 D.C. ammeter and 1 D.C. voltmeter for aux. engine.	Auxiliary panel.
2 D.C. ammeters and 2 D.C. voltmeters for port and starboard generators.	Mechanic's panel.

(4) Cooking

Percolator, roasterette, hot plate.	Galley port side, frame 6.

(5) Lamps

See pages 95 to 98 Incl. for Lamp Data.

(6) Fuses

See pages 99, 100, and 101 for fuse data.

Fig. XXXV-a - Spare Lamp Data: K-3 thru K-6

NAF NO.	TRADE NO.	LAMP TYPE	CP	VOLTS	BASE TYPE	BASE CONT.	LOCATION	NO. REQ'D
	309	S-11	32	28	Cand-Bay	S.C.	Nose Cone	1
	306	S-8	15	28	Cand-Bay	D.C.	Envelope	2
	306	S-8	15	28	Cand-Bay	D.C.	Fins and Tail	4
	306	S-8	15	28	Cand-Bay	D.C.	Outrigger	2
	306	S-8	15	28	Cand-Bay	D.C.	Car-Running	1
	306	S-8	15	28	Cand-Bay	D.C.	Car-Ceiling	5
	1477	T-3	.17A	28	Min-Screw		Flasher Box	1
	1477	T-3	.17A	28	Min-Screw		Pull-Knobs	11
	1477	T-3	.17A	28	Min-Screw		Panel-Inclinator	1 ∕
1068-23	302	T-4½	3	28	Cand-Bay	D.C.	5-0-5-Incl.	1
	304	G-6	6	28	Cand-Bay	D.C.	Pilot's Panel	2
	304	G-6	6	28	Cand-Bay	D.C.	Flight Panel	2
	304	G-6	6	28	Cand-Bay	D.C.	El Indicator	1
	304	G-6	6	28	Cand-Bay	D.C.	Nav-Inst.	1
**			3			S.C.	Nav-Compass	1 ∕∕
**			3			S.C.	Pilot-Compass	1 ∕
1068-20	313	T-3½	.17A	28	Min-Bay	S.C.	Nav-Table	1 ∕
1068-20	313	T-3½	.17A	28	Min-Bay	S.C.	Radio Table	1 ∕
			.9A	22	Pref-Flange	S.C.	Spotlight	1 ∕
*	ST-1220			28			Landing Light	1
	1477	T-3	.17A	28	Min-Screw		Oil-Pressure	2
	304	G-6	6	28	Cand-Bay	D.C.	Mech-Panel	3
***	4618		¼W	125			Aux-Panel	1
***	4618		¼W	125			Hot Plate Jct Box	3
****		PAR-46	5.5A	28	Sealed		Riggers Cabinet	1 ∕

G.A.C.
SK-1-5953

NOTES: ∕ Original Lamp by Equipment manufacturer.
   *   For Grimes Landing Light.
   **   Kollsman Compass Light.
   ***   Bryant #4618 for Bryant Base #9446.
   **** For Grimes Model K-3 portable signal light.

-95-

Fig.XXXV-b - Spare Lamp Data: K-7 and K-8

NAF NO.	TRADE NO.	LAMP TYPE	CP	VOLTS	BASE TYPE	BASE CONT.	LOCATION	NO. REQ'D
	309	S-11	32	28	Cand-Bay	S.C.	Nose Cone	1
	306	S-8	15	28	Cand-Bay	D.C.	Envelope	2
	306	S-8	15	28	Cand-Bay	D.C.	Fins and Tail	4
	305	S-8	15	28	Cand-Bay	S.C.	Car-Running	3
	306	S-8	15	28	Cand-Bay	D.C.	Car-Ceiling	2
1068-20	1477	T-3	.17A	28	Min-Screw		Flasher Box	1
	313	T-3½	.17A	28	Min-Bay	S.C.	Pull-Knobs	11
1068-23	1477	T-3	.17A	28	Min-Screw		Panel-Inclinometer	1 /
	302	T-4½	3	28	Cand-Bay	D.C.	5-0-5-Incl.	1
	304	G-6	6	28	Cand-Bay	D.C.	Pilot's Panel	2
	304	G-6	6	28	Cand-Bay	D.C.	Flight Panel	2
	304	G-6	6	3	Cand-Bay	D.C.	EI Indicator	1
**				3		S.C.	Compass-Rudder	1 /
**						S.C.	Pilot-Compass	1 /
1068-20	313	T-3½	.17A	28	Min-Bay	S.C.	Nav-Table	1 /
1068-23	302	T-4½	3	28	Cand-Bay	D.C.	Radio Table	1 /
*	ST-1220		.9A	22	Pref-Flange	S.C.	Spotlight	1 /
	1477	T-3	.17A	28	Min-Screw		Landing Light	1 /
	304	G-6	6	28	Cand-Bay	D.C.	Oil-Pressure	2
***	4618		½W	125		D.C.	Mech-Panel	3
***	4618		½W	125			Aux.-Panel	1
							Hot Plate Jct Box	3
****		PAR-46	5.5A	28	Sealed		Riggers Cabinet	1 /

NOTES: / Original Lamp by Equipment manufacturer.
    * For Grimes Landing Light.
    ** Kollsman Compass Light.
    *** Bryant #4618 for Bryant Base #19446.
    **** For Grimes Model K-3 portable signal light.

G.A.C.
SK-1-6420

Fig.XXXV-c Spare Lamp Data: K-9 thru K-50

NAF NO.	TRADE NO.	LAMP TYPE	CP	VOLTS	BASE TYPE	BASE CONT.	LOCATION	NO. REQ'D
1068-20	313	T-3¼	.17A	28	Min-Bay	S.C.	Flasher Box	1
1068-20	313	T-3¼	.17A	28	Min-Bay	S.C.	Pull-Knobs	11
1068-20	313	T-3½	.17A	28	Min-Bay	S.C.	Navigator Table	1 ✗
1068-20	313	T-3¾	.17A	28	Min-Bay	S.C.	Mech-Oil Press.	2
1068-20	1477	T-3	.17A	28	Min-Screw		Pilot Panel-Incl.	1 ✗
1068-17	301	T-4½	3	28	Cand-Bay	S.C.	5-0-5 Incl.	1
1068-23	302	T-4½	3	28	Cand-Bay	D.C.	Radio Table	1
1068-18	303	G-6	6	28	Cand-Bay	S.C.	Pilot's Panel	2
1068-18	303	G-6	6	28	Cand-Bay	S.C.	Flight Panel	3
1068-18	303	G-6	6	28	Cand-Bay	S.C.	Mechanic's Panel	3
	305	S-8	15	28	Cand-Bay	S.C.	Car Ceiling	2
	305	S-8	15	28	Cand-Bay	S.C.	Car Running	3
	305	S-8	15	28	Cand-Bay	S.C.	Fins & Tail	4
	305	S-8	15	28	Cand-Bay	S.C.	Envelope	2
	309	S-11	32	28	Cand-Bay	S.C.	Nose Cone	1
			.9A	22	Pref-Flange	S.C.	Spotlight	1 ✗
*	ST-1220			28			Landing Light	1 ✗
**				3			Compass-Pilot	1 ✗
**				3			Compass-Rudder	1 ✗
***	4618		¼W	125			Auxiliary Panel	1
***	4618		¼W	125			Hot Plate Jct Box	3
****		PAR-46	5.5A	28	Sealed		Riggers Cabinet	1 ✗

NOTES: ✗ Original Lamp by Equipment manufacturer.
    * For Grimes #ST-1220 Landing Lite.
    ** Kollsman Compass Light.
    *** Bryant #4618 for Bryant Base #19446.
    **** For Grimes Model K-3 portable signal light.

G.A.C.
SK-1-6404

-97-

Fig. XXXV-d   Spare Lamp Data - K-51 & Fut.

NAF NO.	TRADE NO.	LAMP TYPE	CP	VOLTS	BASE TYPE	BASE CONT.	LOCATION	NO. REQ'D
1068-26	305	S-8	15	28	Cand-Bay	S.C.	Run.Lights-Car	3
	305	S-8	15	28	Cand-Bay	S.C.	" " Env.	3
	305	S-8	15	28	Cand-Bay	S.C.	" " Fin.	3
	305	S-11	32	28	Cand-Bay	S.C.	Nose Cone	1
	305	S-8	15	28	Cand-Bay	S.C.	Dome Lights	2
1068-20	313	T-31		28	Min-Bay	S.C.	Helium Valve Lgt	2
1068-20	313	T-31		28	Min-Bay	S.C.	Navigator Light	1
1068-20	313	T-31		28	Min-Bay	S.C.	Radio Table	1
1068-20	313	T-31		28	Min-Bay	S.C.	Mechanic Panel	3
1068-17		G-6	3	28	Cand-Bay	S.C.	Inclinometer	1
Bryant	3618			125			Hot Plate Junction Box	3*
1192-9				(Neon-lite) 1/4 Watt 24-28	Ultra-Violet-fluorescent		Pilot's Panel	2
1192-9				24-28	Ultra-Violet fluorescent		Mechanics Panel	1
		RP-11	0.9 amps	22	Pref.Flange	S.C.	Spot Lite (Unity)	1
ST1220A			415	24	(100 hour)		Landing Lite (Grimes)	1
1171-2		Par-46	5.5 amp	28	Grimes Sealed Beam		Signal Lite Gun	1
Kollsman #71-900			3				Rudder Compass Light.	1**

*Bryant #4-6/8 lamp for Bryant Base #19446
**Bulb for Kollsman #230B Light Ring

GAC SK-1-7657

Fig. XXXVI-a

ELECTRIC FUSE DATA: K-3 thru K-8

Rating Amps.	Type	Purpose	Location	Cat. No.	NAF Number	No. Reqd.
10	4AG	AC Port Gen.	Auxiliary Panel	1095	1034-4-10	1
10	4AG	AC Stbd Gen.	Auxiliary Panel	1095	1034-4-10	1
10	4AG	AC Aux. Gen.	Auxiliary Panel	1095	1034-4-10	1
10	4AG	AC Spares	Auxiliary Panel	1095	1034-4-10	2
60	HiAmp	DC Aux. Gen.	Aux. Cont. Panel	1235-60	1034-6-60	1
60	HiAmp	DC Aux. Spare	Aux. Cont. Panel	1235-60	1034-6-60	1
50	HiAmp	Engine Gen.	Main-Jct. Box	1235-50	1034-6-50	1
50	HiAmp	Eng. Gen Spare	Main-Jct. Box	1235-50	1034-6-50	1
30	5AG	Radio	Main-Jct Box	1169		1
30	5AG	Radio Spare	Main Jct. Box	1169		1
20	4AG	Spare	Mechanic Panel	1097	1034-4-20	1
20	4AG	Starter Control	Mechanic Panel	1097	1034-4-20	1
20	4AG	Oil-Press	Mechanic Panel	1097	1034-4-20	1
20	4AG	Instruments	Mechanic Panel	1097	1034-4-20	1
20	4AG	Panel Lights	Mechanic Panel	1097	1034-4-20	1
20	4AG	Running Lights	Mechanic Panel	1097	1034-4-20	1
20	4AG	Nav. Lights	Mechanic Panel	1097	1034-4-20	1
20	4AG	Dome Lights	Mechanic Panel	1097	1034-4-20	1
20	4AG	Spare	Mechanic Panel	1097	1034-4-20	1
20	4AG	Spare	Fwd. Sw. Panel	1097	1034-4-20	1
20	4AG	Dome Light	Fwd. Sw. Panel	1097	1034-4-20	1
20	4AG	Panels	Fwd. Sw. Panel	1097	1034-4-20	1
20	4AG	Compass	Fwd. Sw. Panel	1097	1034-4-20	1
20	4AG	Instruments	Fwd. Sw. Panel	1097	1034-4-20	1
30	4AG	Landing Light	Fwd. Sw. Panel	1099	1034-4-30	1
20	4AG	L.L. Motor	Fwd. Sw. Panel	1097	1034-4-20	1
20	4AG	Misc.	Fwd. Sw. Panel	1097	1034-4-20	1
30	4AG	Spare	Fwd. Sw. Panel	1099	1034-4-30	1

NOTE: All catalog numbers by Littelfuse.

G.A.C.
SK-1-6410

Fig. 39

Fig. XXXVI-b

ELECTRIC FUSE DATA: K-9 thru K-50

Rating Amps.	Type	Purpose	Location	Cat. No.	NAF Number	No. Reqd.
10	4AG	AC Port Gen.	Auxiliary Panel	1095	1034-4-10	1
10	4AG	AC-Stbd Gen.	Auxiliary Panel	1095	1034-4-10	1
10	4AG	AC-Aux. Gen.	Auxiliary Panel	1095	1034-4-10	1
10	4AG	AC Spares	Auxiliary Panel	1095	1034-4-10	2
30	5AG	Radio	Main-Jct. Box	1167		1
30	5AG	Radio Spare	Main-Jct. Box	1167		1
10	4AG	Spare	Mechanic Panel	1095	1034-4-10	1
10	4Ag	Starter Control	Mechanic Panel	1095	1034-4-10	1
10	4AG	Oil-Press	Mechanic Panel	1095	1034-4-10	1
10	4AG	Instruments	Mechanic Panel	1095	1034-4-10	1
10	4AG	Panel Lights	Mechanic Panel	1095	1034-4-10	1
10	4AG	Running Lights	Mechanic Panel	1095	1034-4-10	1
10	4AG	Nav. Lights	Mechanic Panel	1095	1034-4-10	1
10	4AG	Galley Light	Mechanic Panel	1095	1034-4-10	1
10	4AG	Spare	Mechanic Panel	1095	1034-4-10	1
5	4AG	Spare	Fwd. Panel	1094	1034-4-5	1
5	4AG	Dome Light	Fwd. Panel	1094	1034-4-5	1
15	4AG	Panels	Fwd. Panel	1096	1034-4-15	1
5	4AG	Compass	Fwd. Panel	1094	1034-4-5	1
5	4AG	Instruments	Fwd. Panel	1094	1034-4-5	1
15	4AG	Landing Light	Fwd. Panel	1096	1034-4-15	1
5	4AG	L.L. Motor	Fwd. Panel	1094	1034-4-5	1
15	4AG	Misc.	Fwd. Panel	1096	1034-4-15	1
15	4AG	Spare	Fwd. Panel	1096	1034-4-15	1

NOTE: All catalog numbers by Littelfuse.

G.A.C.
SK-1-6409

Fig. XXXVI-c

ELECTRIC FUSE DATA: K-51 & Fut.

Rating Amps	Type	Purpose	Location				Cat. No.	NAF No.	No. Req.
10	4AG	Port Generator	AC Aux.Outlet Box				1095	1034-4-10	1
10	4AG	Stbd Generator	"	"	"	"	1095	1034-4-10	1
10	4AG	Converter No.1	"	"	"	"	1095	1034-4-10	1
10	4AG	Converter No.2	"	"	"	"	1095	1034-4-10	1
10	4AG	Spare	"	"	"	"	1095	1034-4-10	1
10	4AG	Oil Pres.Lite	Mechanic's Panel				1095	1034-4-10	1
10	4AG	Instruments	"		"		1095	1034-4-10	1
10	4AG	Running Lights	"		"		1095	1034-4-10	1
10	4AG	Navigation Lgt	"		"		1095	1034-4-10	1
10	4AG	Dome Light	"		"		1095	1034-4-10	1
10	4AG	Spare	"		"		1095	1034-4-10	1
20	4AG	Spare	"		"		1097	1034-4-20	1
20	4AG	IFF	"		"		1097	1034-4-20	1
20	4AG	Navigation Table	"		"		1097	1034-4-20	1
20	4AG	Starter Cont.	"		"		1097	1034-4-20	1
30	4AG	Radio	"		"		1099	1034-4-30	1
30	4AG	Spare	"		"		1099	1034-4-30	1
20	4AG	Spare	"		"		1097	1034-4-20	2
10	4AG	Spare	"		"		1095	1034-4-10	2
5	4AG	Spare	Fwd.SW & Fuse Pan.				1094	1034-4-5	1
5	4AG	Dome	"	"	"	"	1094	1034-4-5	1
5	4AG	Compass	"	"	"	"	1094	1034-4-5	1
5	4AG	Instruments	"	"	"	"	1094	1034-4-5	1
5	4AG	L.L. Motor	"	"	"	"	1094	1034-4-5	1
5	4AG	U.V.Light	"	"	"	"	1094	1034-4-5	1
15	4AG	Landing Light	"	"	"	"	1096	1034-4-15	1
15	4AG	Miscellaneous	"	"	"	"	1096	1034-4-15	1
15	4AG	Spare	"	"	"	"	1096	1034-4-15	1
50	5AG	Spare	Main Junc. Box				1169		1
50	5AG	MAD	"	"		"	1169		1
30	5AG	Spare	"	"		"	1167		1
30	5AG	Radar	"	"		"	1167		1

NOTE: All Catalog Numbers by Littlefuse, Inc.   GAC SK-1-7658

E. LAWRANCE AUXILIARY GASOLINE POWERED ELECTRIC GENERATOR

    (1) Specifications of the Lawrance Auxiliary Power Unit Model 30 C-2:

No. of Cylinders	2
Ignition	Dual
Horsepower	14.5
Output DC (Continuous)	5 KW
Weight (pounds)	213
Fuel Octane	91-100
RPM	4100
Output (5 mins.cont.)	7.5 KW (resting 30 minutes with an 86 amp.load of 28.1 volts.)

    (2) Preparations for starting

        Before attempting to start the engine for the first time, the following checks should be made:

(a) At least three (3) gallons of lubrication oil Navy Specification 1065 to 1080 should be placed in the oil tank.

(b) See that 24 volts of battery are across line and that the main line switches for auxiliary power plant are in "off" position.

(c) Inspect magneto ground wires for proper connection.

    Notice: Press in on automatic over-speed cut out button to make sure switch is in operating position.

(d) Fuel tank should contain 91 octane gasoline. Open valves and check engine dribble valve for flooding.

(e) By aid of the hand crank, turn the engine through two or three revolutions. If abnormal effort is required, remove a spark plug from each cylinder to make sure liquid has not collected in the combustion chamber.

    This procedure should be followed whenever the engine has been idle for a week or more. (See Navy Spec. AN9505a for preparation for storage instructions).

ITEM	DESCRIPTION
1	Lawrance Generator
2	Mount - Auxiliary Generator
3	Auxiliary Blower - Homelite
4	Ventilation Control Box
5	Duct - Air Intake
6	Air Outlet & Exhaust Assembly
7	Oil Pressure Line
8	Fuel Line
9	Oil Line - To Engine
10	Oil Line - Return
11	Oil Tank Vent Line
12	Alternator Box
13	Alternators
14	Air Intake - Alternators
15	Oil Tank
16	Support Bracket - Oil Tank
17	Drain Tube Assembly
18	D.C. Box
19	A.C. Box
20	D.C. Voltmeter 0-35 V
21	Ignition Switch
22	Oil Temp. Gage 0-120°C.
23	A.C. Voltmeter 0-150-V
24	D.C. Ammeter 0-480 Amps.
25	Relay Switch
26	Starter Switch
27	Cylinder Temp. Gage
28	Oil Heater Switch
29	Breaker Switch Alt. #2
30	Breaker Switch Alt. #1
31	Selector Switch
32	Switch - Alt.#2 - On-Off
33	Switch-Alternator #1 On-Off
34	Voltage Regulator
35	Meter Mounting Box
36	Oil Pressure Gage
37	Groundwire
38	Lead to Oil Temperature
39	Lead for Cooker A.C.
40	Lead for Radio A.C.
41	Lead for Radar A.C.
42	Lead to Oil Heater D.C.
43	Lead to Magneto
44	Lead to Voltage Regulator
45	Lead from Alt. #2 A.C.
46	Lead from Alt. #1 A.C.
47	Lead to Alt. #2 D.C.
48	Lead to Alt. #1 D.C.
49	Power Lead D.C.
50	Thermocouple Lead
51	Lead to Battery

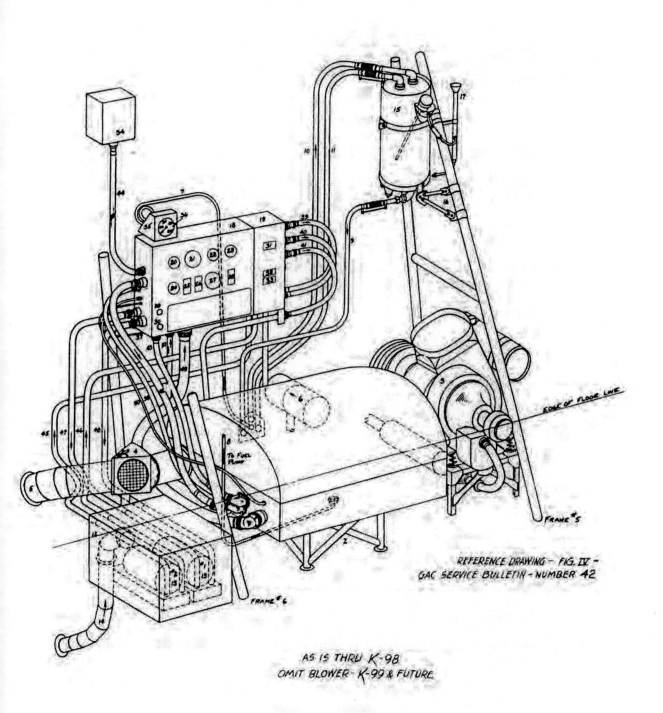

EDGE OF FLOOR LINE

FRAME #5

FRAME #6

REFERENCE DRAWING – FIG. IV –
GAC SERVICE BULLETIN – NUMBER 42

TO FUEL PUMP

AS IS THRU K-98
OMIT BLOWER – K-99 & FUTURE

Fig. XXXVII

AUXILIARY GENERATOR & BLOWER

(3) <u>Starting</u>

After the above preparations, the engine may be started in the following manner:

(a) Turn fuel valve to "ON."

(b) Turn oil valve to "ON."

(c) Close main line switch for auxiliary power plant. See that generator lead is connected.

(d) Turn starter switch to "ON." Allow starter to prime engine with fuel and oil pump with oil.

(e) Turn ignition switch to "BOTH" when oil pressure gauge registers pressure.

(f) Turn starter switch to "OFF" as soon as engine fires.

(g) As soon as engine starts, observe the oil pressure gauge and shut engine off immediately if pressure is not indicated. Normal oil pressure is 55-65 lbs. per sq. inch.

(4) <u>Manual Starting</u>

If no 24-volt battery source is available, the engine may be started with the hand starting drum.

(a) Loosen the two Dzus fasteners holding the starter hole cover and remove the cover plate.

(b) Insert the starting drum shaft until it engages the engine crankshaft nut at the generator end.

(c) Wrap the rope around the drum so that it will turn counter-clockwise when facing the generator end of the engine.

(d) Maintain tension on the starter rope to keep the drum engaged.

(e) Turn fuel valve, oil valve, and ignition switch to "ON" position.

(f) Pull rope thru to spin engine crankshaft and start engine.

(g) Repeat the process if the engine does not start at first pull.

(5) Warm Up

When the operating temperature is below 21°C the engine will idle at about 1800 RPM after starting. As the oil warms, the engine speed will gradually increase to 4200 RPM (no load). The governor is adjusted at the factory to operate betweeen 4000 (full load) and 4200 RPM (No load). During warm-up the engine oil heater should be turned to "ON." Normal operating oil-in temperature should be about 60°C. and should not be permitted to exceed 87°C. DO NOT USE OIL HEATER BEFORE STARTING ENGINE.

(6) Loading

Load may be applied to generator as soon as the engine comes up to speed.

(7) Overload Caution

The generator is rated at 5 K.W. (175 amp.) for continuous operation. It has an overload capacity of 7.5 K.W. (263 amp.) for a 5 minute period.

CAUTION: DO NOT operate the power plant above the normal 5 K.W. load for more than five minutes at a time. Allow 10 minutes at not more than 50% load (85 amp.) between overload periods for the generator to cool.

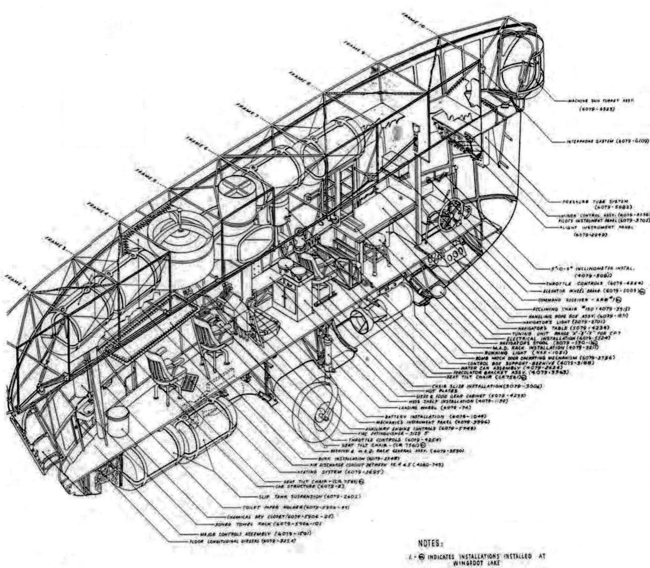

MACHINE GUN TURRET ASSY.
(6079-6825)

INTERPHONE SYSTEM (6079-6109)

PRESSURE TUBE SYSTEM
(6079-5882)

MINOR CONTROL ASSY. (6079-9750)
PILOTS INSTRUMENT PANEL (6079-3702)
FLIGHT INSTRUMENT PANEL
(6079-0990)

5°O-5° INCLINOMETER INSTAL.
(4079-8082)
THROTTLE CONTROLS (6079-4264)
ELEVATOR WHEEL BRAKE (6079-5001)
COMMAND RECEIVER - ARB 4 0
RECLINING CHAIR #150 (4079-2513)
HANDLING ROPE BOX ASSY (6079-1871)
NAVIGATOR'S LIGHT (6079-2701)
NAVIGATOR'S TABLE (5079-4234)
TUNING UNIT RANGE 2'-7"-7" FOR CRT
ELECTRICAL INSTALLATION (6079-5524)
NAVIGATOR'S STOOL (6079-150-10)
RUNNING LIGHT (R45-1021)
M.A.D. RACK INSTALLATION (4079-327)
BOMB HATCH DOOR OMITTING MECHANISM (6079-2736)
CONTROL BOX SUPPORT-SLEEVE (4079-3108)
WATER CAN ASSEMBLY (6079-2625)
PERCOLATOR BRACKET ASSY. (4079-3763)
SEAT TILT CHAIR (CR 7560)
CHAIR SLIDE INSTALLATION (5079-3004)
HOT PLATES
DISH & FOOD GEAR CABINET (6079-4233)
MESS SHELF INSTALLATION (6079-1130)
LANDING WHEEL (6079-74)
BATTERY INSTALLATION (6079-1049)
MECHANICS INSTRUMENT PANEL (6079-3996)
AUXILIARY ENGINE CONTROLS (6079-9749)
FIRE EXTINGUISHER - 3123 0
THROTTLE CONTROLS (6079-9264)
SEAT TILT CHAIR (CR 7560) 0
RECEIVER & M.A.D. RACK GENERAL ASSY. (6079-3550)
BUNK INSTALLATION (6079-2248)
AIR EXCHANGE CIRCUIT BETWEEN FR.4 & 5 (4060-745)
HEATING SYSTEM (6079-2605)
SEAT TILT CHAIR - (CR 7560) 0
CAR STRUCTURE (6079-8)
SLIP TANK SUSPENSION (6079-2402)
TOILET PAPER HOLDER (6079-2906-21)
CHEMICAL DRY CLOSET (6079-2906-21)
SOHIO TOWEL RACK (6079-2906-101)
MAJOR CONTROLS ASSEMBLY (6079-1501)
FLOOR LONGITUDINAL GIRDERS (6079-3254)

NOTES:
1. ⊙ INDICATES INSTALLATIONS INSTALLED AT WINGFOOT LAKE
2. VIEWS FROM CENTER OF SHIP-LOOKING OUTBOARD

SPLIT VIEW OF CONTROL CAR
K-123 and Future
K-TYPE AIRSHIP

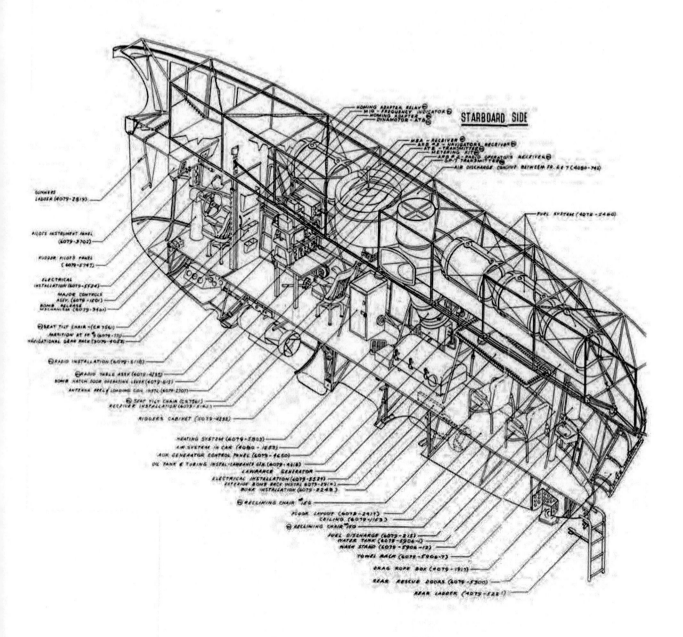

STARBOARD SIDE

HOMING ADAPTER RELAY
MED. FREQUENCY INDICATOR
HOMING ADAPTER
DYNAMOTOR (4718)

MSA - RECEIVER
ARK 2S - NAVIGATORS RECEIVER
ARN-1 TRANSMITTER & RECEIVING UNITS
ARN-7 RADIO OPERATORS RECEIVER
AIR DISCHARGE CONDUIT BETWEEN FR. 6 & 7 (4080-74)

GUNNERS
LADDER (4079-2519)

FUEL SYSTEM (4079-2460)

PILOTS INSTRUMENT PANEL
(4079-3702)

RUDDER PILOTS PANEL
(4079-2745)

ELECTRICAL
INSTALLATION (4079-5524)
MAJOR CONTROLS
ASSY. (4079-1201)
BOMB RELEASE
MECHANISM (4079-3461)

SEAT TILT CHAIR (CM 756)
PARTITION AT FR. 5 (4079-17)
NAVIGATIONAL GEAR RACK (3079-4022)

RADIO INSTALLATION (4079-5118)
RADIO TABLE ASSY. (4079-4215)
BOMB HATCH DOOR OPERATING LEVER (4079-615)
ANTENNA RELAY LOADING COIL INSTL (4079-2301)
SEAT TILT CHAIR (CM756)
RECEIVER INSTALLATION (4079-514)
RIGGERS CABINET (5079-4252)

HEATING SYSTEM (4079-5802)
AIR SYSTEM IN CAR (4080-1253)
AIR GENERATOR CONTROL PANEL (4079-4650)
OIL TANK & TUBING INSTAL-AMBULANCE GEN (4079-4518)
AMBULANCE GENERATOR
ELECTRICAL INSTALLATION (4079-5529)
EXTERIOR BOMB RACK INSTAL (4079-4514)
BOMB INSTALLATION (4079-2248)

RECLINING CHAIR #40
FLOOR LAYOUT (4079-2417)
CEILING (4079-4165)
RECLINING CHAIR #20
FUEL DISCHARGE (4079-215)
WATER TANK (4079-5906-1)
WASH STAND (4079-5906-13)
TOWEL RACK (4079-5906-7)
DRAG ROPE BOX (4079-1913)
REAR RESCUE DOORS (4079-5301)
REAR LADDER (4079-523)

V-a

-108-

C - CONTINOUS
M - MOMENTARY (5 MIN OR LESS)
X - OFF
- NAVY FURNISHED
- DURATION OF FLIGHT

TYPE OF EQUIPMENT	MANUFACTURER & PART DESIGNATION	NO OF UNITS	AMPERES PER UNIT	DURATION OF OPERATION	TYPE OF OPERATION (M OR C)	TOTAL AMPERE LOADING DURING OPER			
						NORMAL ANCHOR	NORMAL CRUISING	NIGHT CRUISING	BATTLE ACTION
POWER SOURCE & CONTROLS									
GENERATORS - OUTRIGGER	*Eclipse 584-1A-NXA-2X	2	DC 251 @ 28.5 Volts]Cont. Full AC		*C				
CONTROL - BOX	*Eclipse NP-1D	2							
AUXILIARY - POWER UNIT	*Lawrance-Navy Type One	1							
ENGINE	*Model 300-1	1							
GENERATOR	*Model 2CM41A4	1	150A @ 30 V.Cont. as required		M or C				
CONTROL BOX	*G.E.- 3CBD1-A11	1							
RELAY - REV. CURRENT	*G.E. - 3CTR72A1	1							
STARTER - CONTACTOR	*G.E. - 3CTRT2B1	1							
BATTERIES	*N.A.F. 1062-34	2	34 Ampere Hrs.						
CONVERTERS	*Eclipse - 900-1-B	2	62 A., 24-26-V.	As required	C	See Note#**	62.0	62.0	62.0
A - PERSONNEL EQUIPMENT									
GRILL - STOVE - OVEN	GE Grill	1	6.7A @ 120 V.AC	3 to 4 hrs/day	C	X	6.7 AC	6.7 AC	x
PERCOLATOR	Manning Bowman #494	1	3.0A @ 120 V.AC	3 to 5 hrs/day	C	X	3.0 AC	3.0 AC	x
ROASTERETTE	Everhot	1	3.0A @ 120 V.AC	2 to 3 hrs/day	C	X	3.0 AC	3.0 AC	x
TOASTER									
B - ARMAMENT									
BOMB -DOOR									
SOUNDEBUOY		1	4.0 A @ 24 V.	While on patrol	C	X	4.0	4.0	4.0
C - ENGINE									
HEATER - OIL SERVICE TANK	E.L.Weigand - Navy Type C	2	1000W - 120 V.	(Shore Connection)					
HEATER - AUXILIARY UNIT	Furnished with Lawrance Unit	1	10A @ 24 Volts	As required	C	X	10.0	10.0	10.0
HEATER - ENGINE									
STARTER	*Eclipse, Series 11,Type 569	2	300 A @ 24 V.	(While starting Engine)	M				
STARTER - SOLENOID SWITCH	*Eclipse Type 518 Model 2A	2	1 A @ 28 V.	" " "	M				
MESHING - SOLENOID DEVICE	*Eclipse, Series 11,Type 500	2		" " "	M				
BOOSTER COIL	*Eclipse,Type 513, Model 7A	2	1.6 A @ 18 V.	" " "	M				
TRANSFER PUMPS - FUEL									
E - LIGHTING									
LANDING LIGHT	Grimes Mfg.Co. 8T 1220 A	1	10A @ 24 V.	Night Landing Only	C	X	X	10.0	x
SPOTLIGHT	Unity Mft.Co. Deluxe 6½" lens	1	5.5A A 28 V.	As required	C	X	X	5.5	x
RUNNING LIGHTS - CAR	GAC per Dwg. #2079-1505	3	0.6A @ 28 V.	Night operation only	C	X	X	1.8	1.8
RUNNING LIGHTS - ENVELOPE	GAC See Note #2 ***	7	0.6 A @ 28 V.	" " "	C	X	X	4.2	4.2
INDICATOR LIGHTS	Grimes #A2328	5	0.17 A @ 28 V.	As required	C	X	0.85	0.85	0.85
C - ENGINE									
HEATER - OIL SERVICE TANK	E.L.Weigand - Navy Type C	2	1000W - 120 V.	(Shore Connection)					
HEATER - AUXILIARY UNIT	Furnished with Lawrance Unit	1	10A @ 24 Volts	As required	C	X	10.0	10.0	10.0
HEATER - ENGINE									
STARTER	*Eclipse, Series 11,Type 569	2	300 A @ 24 V.	(While starting Engine)	M				
STARTER - SOLENOID SWITCH	*Eclipse Type 518 Model 2A	2	1 A @ 28 V.	" " "	M				
MESHING - SOLENOID DEVICE	*Eclipse, Series 11,Type 500	2		" " "	M				
BOOSTER COIL	*Eclipse,Type 513, Model 7A	2	1.6 A @ 18 V.	" " "	M				
TRANSFER PUMPS - FUEL									
E - LIGHTING									
LANDING LIGHT	Grimes Mfg.Co. 8T 1220 A	1	10A @ 24 V.	Night Landing Only	C	X	X	10.0	x
SPOTLIGHT	Unity Mft.Co. Deluxe 6½" lens	1	5.5A A 28 V.	As required	C	X	X	5.5	x
RUNNING LIGHTS - CAR	GAC per Dwg. #2079-1505	3	0.6A @ 28 V.	Night operation only	C	X	X	1.8	1.8
RUNNING LIGHTS - ENVELOPE	GAC See Note #2 ***	7	0.6 A @ 28 V.	" " "	C	X	X	4.2	4.2
INDICATOR LIGHTS	Grimes #A2328	5	0.17 A @ 28 V.	As required	C	X	0.85	0.85	0.85
SIGNAL LIGHT	Grimes K-3, NAF 1171-2	1	5.3A @ 24 V.	" "	M	5.3	5.3	5.3	5.3
CAR LIGHTING	GAC	1	0.6 @ 24 V.	" "	C	1.2	1.2	1.2	1.2
NAVIGATOR'S LIGHT	Fairchild "Moonglow"	1	0.2 A @ 24 V.	" "	C	0.2	0.2	0.2	0.2
RADIO TABLE LIGHT	GAC	1	0.17 A @ 24 V.	" "	C	0.17	0.17	0.17	0.17
PANEL - INCANDESCENT	GAC	2	0.17 A @ 24 V.	" "	C	X	0.34	0.34	0.34
PANEL - ULTRA VIOLET	NAF 1192-1	3	0.2 A @ 24 V.	" "	C	0.6	0.6	0.6	0.6
F - RADIO									
MAIN TRANSMITTER	Westinghouse GP-7	1	AC 5.8A @ 28V	As required	C	5.8 AC	5.8 AC	5.8 AC	5.8 AC
TRANSMIT				Same					
STANDBY				Same	**				
MAIN RECEIVER	Western Electric RU-19	1	Not Available	**					
INTRA-SQUAD TRANSMITTER	Western Electric GR-12	1)							
TRANSMIT									
STANDBY	See Note #3 ***	}	7.0 A @ 26 V.	**	C	7.0	7.0	7.0	7.0
INTRA-SQUAD RECEIVER	Western Electric RU-17	1)							
MARKER BEACON RECEIVER									
INTERPHONE	Magnavox Co. R1240	1	2.5 A. 24 V.	**	C	2.5	2.5	2.5	2.5
RADAR	"	1	AC 9.5 @ 28V	**	C	X	AC 9.5	AC 9.5	AC 9.5
DIRECTION FINDER	*30A - DZ-2A	1	1.6 A @ 26 V.	** See Note #4 ***	C	X	1.6	1.6	1.6
FREQUENCY INDICATOR	*Bendix Radio - LM7	1	1.25 A @ 26 V.	As required	M	1.25	1.25	1.25	1.25
HOMING EQUIPMENT	Western Electric-ZB1 or ZB3	1	1.25 A @ 25 V.	" "	M		1.25	1.25	1.25
I.F.F. SYSTEM	*ABK	1	5.5 A @ 26 V.	**	C	X	5.5	5.5	5.5
M.A.D. SYSTEM	*Mark IV	1	15 A @ 24 V.	**	C	X	15.0	15.0	15.0
MISC. RADIO EQUIPMENT									

RUNNING LIGHTS - CAR	GAC per Dwg. #3079-1505	3	0.6A @ 28 V.	Night operation only	C	x			
RUNNING LIGHTS - ENVELOPE	GAC See Note #2 ***	7	0.6 A @ 28 V.	" " "	C	x	x	4.2	4.2
INDICATOR LIGHTS	Grimes #A2328	6	0.17 A @ 28 V.	As required	C	x	0.85	0.85	0.85

C - ENGINE

HEATER - OIL SERVICE TANK	E.L.Weigand - Navy Type C	2	1000W - 120 V.	(Shore Connection)					
HEATER - AUXILIARY UNIT	Furnished with Lawrance Unit	1	10A @ 24 Volts	As required	C	x	10.0	10.0	10.0
HEATER - ENGINE									
STARTER	*Eclipse, Series 11, Type 522 Mod.4J	2	300 A @ 24 V.	(While starting Engine)	M				
STARTER - SOLENOID SWITCH	*Eclipse Type 516 Model 2A	2	1 A @ 28 V.	" " "	M				
MESHING - SOLENOID DEVICE	*Eclipse, Series 11, Type 500 Mod.4J	2		" " "	M				
BOOSTER COIL	*Eclipse, Type 513, Model 7A	2	1.8 A @ 18 V.	" " "	M				
TRANSFER PUMPS - FUEL									

E - LIGHTING

LANDING LIGHT	Grimes Mfg.Co. 8T 1220 A	1	10A @ 24 V.	Night Landing Only	C	x	x	10.0	x
SPOTLIGHT	Unity Mfg.Co. Deluxe 6½" lens	1	5.5A A @ 28 V.	As required	C	x	x	5.5	x
RUNNING LIGHTS - CAR	GAC per Dwg. #3079-1505	3	0.6A @ 28 V.	Night operation only	C	x	x	1.8	1.8
RUNNING LIGHTS - ENVELOPE	GAC See Note #2 ***	7	0.6 A @ 28 V.	" " "	C	x	x	4.2	4.2
INDICATOR LIGHTS	Grimes #A2328	6	0.17 A @ 28 V.	As required	C	x	0.85	0.85	0.85
SIGNAL LIGHT	Grimes K-3, NAF 1171-2	1	5.3A @ 24 V.	" "	M	5.3	5.3	5.3	5.3
CAR LIGHTING	GAC	2	0.6 A @ 24 V.	" "	C	1.2	1.2	1.2	1.2
NAVIGATOR'S LIGHT	Fairchild "Moonglow"	1	0.2 A @ 24 V.	" "	C	0.2	0.2	0.2	0.2
RADIO TABLE LIGHT	GAC	1	0.17 A @ 24 V.	" "	C	0.17	0.17	0.17	0.17
PANEL - INCANDESCENT	GAC	2	0.17 A @ 24 V.	" "	C	x	0.34	0.34	0.34
PANEL - ULTRA VIOLET	NAF 1192-1	3	0.2 A @ 24 V.	" "	C	0.6	0.6	0.6	0.6

F - RADIO

MAIN TRANSMITTER	Westinghouse GP-7	1	AC 5.8A @ 28V	As required	C	5.8 AC	5.8 AC	5.8 AC	5.8 AC
TRANSMIT			Same						
STANDBY			Same	**					
MAIN RECEIVER	*Western Electric RU-19	1	Not Available	**					
INTRA-SQUAD TRANSMITTER	*Western Electric GR-12	1)							
TRANSMIT		}							
STANDBY	See Note #3 ***	}	7.0 A @ 28 V.	**	C	7.0	7.0	7.0	7.0
INTRA-SQUAD RECEIVER	*Western Electric RU-17	1)							
MARKER BEACON RECEIVER									
INTERPHONE	Magnavox Co. R1240	1	2.5 A. 24 V.	**	C	2.5	2.5	2.5	2.5
RADAR	"	1	AC 5.8A @ 28V	**	C	x	AC 5.8	AC 5.8	AC 5.8
DIRECTION FINDER	*GA - DZ-2A	1	1.5 A @ 26 V.	** See Note #4 ***	C	x	1.5	1.5	1.5
FREQUENCY INDICATOR	*Bendix Radio - LM7	1	1.25 A @ 28 V.	As required	M	1.25	1.25	1.25	1.25
HOMING EQUIPMENT	*Western Electric-ZB1 or ZB3	1	1.25 A @ 28 V.	" "	M	x	1.25	1.25	1.25
I.F.F. SYSTEM	*ABK	1	5.5 A @ 28 V.	**	C	x	5.5	5.5	5.5
M.A.D. SYSTEM	*Mark IV	1	15 A @ 24 V.	**	C	x	15.0	15.0	15.0
MISC. RADIO EQUIPMENT									

F - RADIO

MAIN TRANSMITTER	Westinghouse GP-7	1	AC 5.8A @ 28V	As required	C	5.8 AC	5.8 AC	5.8 AC	5.8 AC
TRANSMIT			Same						
STANDBY			Same	**					
MAIN RECEIVER	*Western Electric RU-19	1	Not Available	**					
INTRA-SQUAD TRANSMITTER	*Western Electric GR-12	1)							
TRANSMIT		}							
STANDBY	See Note #3 ***	}	7.0 A @ 28 V.	**	C	7.0	7.0	7.0	7.0
INTRA-SQUAD RECEIVER	*Western Electric RU-17	1)							
MARKER BEACON RECEIVER									
INTERPHONE	Magnavox Co. R1240	1	2.5 A. 24 V.	**	C	2.5	2.5	2.5	2.5
RADAR	"	1	AC 5.8A @ 28V	**	C	x	AC 5.8	AC 5.8	AC 5.8
DIRECTION FINDER	*GA - DZ-2A	1	1.5 A @ 26 V.	** See Note #4 ***	C	x	1.5	1.5	1.5
FREQUENCY INDICATOR	*Bendix Radio - LM7	1	1.25 A @ 28 V.	As required	M	1.25	1.25	1.25	1.25
HOMING EQUIPMENT	*Western Electric-ZB1 or ZB3	1	1.25 A @ 28 V.	" "	M	x	1.25	1.25	1.25
I.F.F. SYSTEM	*ABK	1	5.5 A @ 28 V.	**	C	x	5.5	5.5	5A
M.A.D. SYSTEM	*Mark IV	1	15 A @ 24 V.	**	C	x	15.0	15.0	15.0
MISC. RADIO EQUIPMENT									

G - MISCELLANEOUS

MAPPING CAMERA									
INSTRUMENTS	Operating Current	Lot	4 A @ 28 Volts	**	C	x	4.0	4.0	4.0

REMARKS

REMARKS: Power Source	Continuous	Momentary						
Outrigger Generator	80 amps.	50 amps.	TOTAL CONTINUOUS LOAD	11.67	122.06	143.56	127.52
Lawrance Generator	147 amps.	250 amps.	ADDITIONAL MOMENTARY LOAD	6.55	7.60	7.80	7.80
	217 amps.	300 amps.	TOTAL LOAD	18.22	129.66	151.36	135.32

Note #1. Converter used to supply A.C.Load. A.C. loads not included in totals since Converter D.C. load is shown.

Note #2. Per G.A.C. Drawings #3080-85, 61071-796, & 61021-782.

Note #3. Standby and Receive 5.6A @ 28 Volts, and 7.0 A on Transmit. **

Note #4. Momentary 3.5 A relay current.

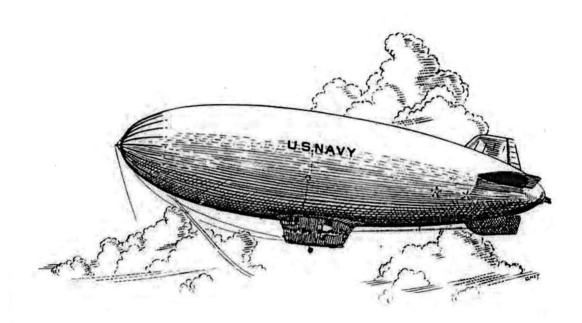

CPSIA information can be obtained at www.ICGtesting.com
Printed in the USA
BVOW04s1410220216

437624BV00005B/47/P